A Glimpse at Humor In the Prophetic Sunnah

AL-RAHMANIYYAH
PRESS

A Glimpse at Humor
In the
Prophetic Sunnah

Abu Al-Hasan Malik Al-Akhdar

ISBN: 979-8-89480-291-6

Published by:

Al-Rahmaniyyah Press
PO Box 8671 Turnersville, NJ 08012 U.S.A.
Electronic mail: editor@alrahmaniyyah.com

Reviewed by Abu Suhayl Anwar Wright
Edited by Al-Rahmaniyyah Press
Proofread by Abu Aasiyah Habeeb Luis Herrera
Cover Art by Al-Rahmaniyyah Press

Allah says:

﴿ وَأَنَّهُ هُوَ أَضْحَكَ وَأَبْكَىٰ ﴾

"And that it is He Who makes one laugh and cry." [*Al-Najm* 53:43]

Table of Contents

Introduction

Indeed, all praise is for Allah. We praise Him and seek His aid, help, and forgiveness. We seek refuge in Allah from the evil within ourselves and the evil of our actions. Whoever Allah guides cannot be led astray, and whoever Allah misguides cannot be guided. I bear witness that there is nothing worthy of worship except for Allah, with no partner. And I bear witness that Muhammad ﷺ is His servant and Messenger.

يَٰٓأَيُّهَا ٱلَّذِينَ ءَامَنُواْ ٱتَّقُواْ ٱللَّهَ حَقَّ تُقَاتِهِۦ وَلَا تَمُوتُنَّ إِلَّا وَأَنتُم مُّسْلِمُونَ

"O you who believe, fear Allah as He should be feared and do not die except as Muslims."

[*Ali-'Imran* 3:102]

يَٰٓأَيُّهَا ٱلنَّاسُ ٱتَّقُواْ رَبَّكُمُ ٱلَّذِى خَلَقَكُم مِّن نَّفْسٍ وَٰحِدَةٍ وَخَلَقَ مِنْهَا زَوْجَهَا وَبَثَّ مِنْهُمَا رِجَالًا كَثِيرًا وَنِسَآءً ۚ وَٱتَّقُواْ ٱللَّهَ ٱلَّذِى تَسَآءَلُونَ بِهِۦ وَٱلْأَرْحَامَ ۚ إِنَّ ٱللَّهَ كَانَ عَلَيْكُمْ رَقِيبًا

"O people, fear your Lord, who created you from a single soul and created from this soul its mate and sent forth from the two of them many men and women. And fear your Lord through whom you demand your mutual rights, and [fear Allah] concerning kinship ties. Indeed, Allah is always observing you."

[*Al-Nisa'* 4:1]

بِسْمِ اللَّهِ الَّذِينَ ءَامَنُوا اتَّقُوا اللَّهَ وَقُولُوا قَوْلًا سَدِيدًا ٧٠ يُصْلِحْ لَكُمْ
أَعْمَالَكُمْ وَيَغْفِرْ لَكُمْ ذُنُوبَكُمْ وَمَن يُطِعِ اللَّهَ وَرَسُولَهُ فَقَدْ فَازَ فَوْزًا
عَظِيمًا ٧١ ۝

"O you who believe, fear Allah and speak directly and
forthright. He will rectify your affairs and forgive you
of your sins. And whoever obeys Allah and His
Messenger has [truly] achieved a great achievement."

[*Al-Ahzab* 33:70-71]

To proceed:

The most truthful speech is the speech of Allah, and the best
guidance is the guidance of Muhammad ﷺ. The
most evil of affairs are newly invented matters, which are
religious innovations (*bid'ah*). Every religious innovation
(*bid'ah*) is misguidance, and all misguidance is in the Hellfire.

Recently, I heard a discussion about the aftermath of the
Charlie Hebdo case in Paris. One participant in this discussion,
out of blatant ignorance, claimed that Muslims were angered
and offended because Islam frowns upon laughter and humor.
After hearing such a bald-faced lie, I referred to some chapters
I had translated from *Al-Shama'il Al-Muhammadiyyah* (*The
Characteristics of the Prophet Muhammad*) by the scholar of *hadith*
Abu 'Isa Muhammad b. 'Isa Al-Tirmidhi—with commentary
from *Al-Muhaddith* Muhammad Nasir Al-Din Al-Albani.

This classical compilation comprehensively examines Prophet
Muhammad's ﷺ life, encompassing his physical

appearance, daily habits, devotional practices, and personality. Notably, it explores his humorous side, highlighting the jokes and laughter he shared with his family and companions. Many in the West misunderstand the Prophet's life. They believe, based on limited knowledge, that Islam forbids humor. This is erroneous. Prophet Muhammad's ﷺ perfect character and comprehensive message made it natural for him to use humor in conveying his message. This led several *hadith* scholars to gather such traditions in their writings, including:

- *Imam* Al-Bukhari in *Al-Adab Al-Mufrad*: "The Chapter of Joking and Laughter"

- *Imam* Al-Tirmidhi in *Al-Jami*: "The Chapter of What Has Been Related Regarding Joking"

- *Imam* Abu Dawud in *Al-Sunan*: "What has Been Related Regarding the Description of the Prophet's Joking"

- *Imams* Ibn Majah in *Al-Sunan* and Al-Darimi in *Al-Musnad*: "The Chapter of Joking"

- *Imam* Ibn Al-Hibban in *Al-Sahih*: "The Chapter of Joking and Laughter"

Under this heading, Ibn Hibban clarifies that humor is permissible between brothers as long as it does not violate the Book and the *Sunnah*. [1]

Of course, this does not detract from the seriousness of the Prophet's ﷺ mission. While he used humor in certain circumstances, as we will explore, it was always with a

---

[1] Refer to *Sahih Ibn Hibban* (13/106)

wise purpose: to comfort the grieving, extend warmth and affection to his loved ones, and bring joy to children.

The Prophet's occasional humor serves an obvious purpose and rebukes those who indulge in excessive joking, bordering on buffoonery. Unfortunately, some callers and preachers undermine the seriousness of their message by filling their sermons and lessons with excessive jokes and stories. Perhaps even more concerning is a group of Muslim comedians who launched a nationwide tour explicitly intended to showcase their comedic talents as "a gift from Allah." This approach raises serious questions about the appropriateness of exploiting religion for laughs and giggles.

Concerning these two extremes, the noble *Shaykh* Salih Al-Fawzan was asked, "What is the extent of joking with one's companions in gatherings and on travels, O *Shaykh*? Also, is there any objection to a person jesting, joking, and laughing excessively in public?" The *Shaykh* responded, "There is nothing inherently wrong with joking occasionally, as long as one avoids mockery, ridicule, or anything religiously forbidden. The Prophet ﷺ occasionally joked, but always with truthfulness. However, being known as a jokester or making it a primary focus is harmful. Such behavior diminishes one's stature and respect in the eyes of others, and it carries the risk of slipping into forbidden speech."[1] In these pages, we hope to prove, Allah willing, that moderation remains the correct path, avoiding both extremes. As *Shaykh* Muhammad b. Salih Al-'Uthaymin said, "A person should be cautious of excessive joking, as it often leads to error. As the saying goes, 'Joking in

---

[1] See:
http://www.sunnahpublishing.net/audio/fawzaanhukumalmezaah.mp3

speech is like salt in food.' Without it, the food is bland. Too much spoils it. Therefore, be moderate. Do not joke about serious matters, nor be serious in matters of jest. A wise person acts appropriately in each situation."[1]

After referring to chapters from *Al-Shama'il Al-Muhammadiyyah*, I felt it worthwhile to compile additional authentic narrations from various sources, highlighting the Prophet's humorous interactions with his family and companions. If I thought a narration needed clarification, I added brief commentary from well-known *hadith* scholars. I have titled this collection: *A Glimpse at Humor in the Prophetic Sunnah*. I pray Allah allows readers to benefit from the illustrious example of His Messenger ﷺ. Indeed, Allah has power over all things.

Abu Al-Hasan Malik Al-Akhdar

---

[1] *Sharh Bulugh Al-Maram* (15/542)

Introduction to the Second Edition

Twelve years ago, I compiled a collection of Prophetic traditions highlighting the Prophet's humor to familiarize Western readers with his true character. After the book went out of print, many requested a second edition. This publication fulfills their wishes.

In this new edition, I included additional sections, such as one on laughter, along with several new narrations showing the humor of the companions and the scholars of the *Sunnah*. I also revised the text and translation of traditions, improving clarity and accuracy.

I pray this work, *A Glimpse at Humor in the Prophetic Sunnah*, continues illuminating the Prophet's illustrious example. May Allah make it a source of benefit for Islam and the Muslims.

Abu Al-Hasan Malik Al-Akhdar
1 Dhu Al-Hijjah 1445 AH
Casablanca, Morocco

Section One: Laughter and Joking in the Islamic Legislation

Laughter (الضحك) is defined as "the appearance of teeth when experiencing joy and happiness."[1] And because the incisors are revealed during laughter, they are called (الضواحك) in Arabic.[2]

Allah says in His Noble Book,

$$ \text{﴿ وَأَنَّهُ هُوَ أَضْحَكَ وَأَبْكَىٰ ﴾} $$

"And that it is He Who makes one laugh and cry." [Al-Najm 53:43]

Concerning this verse, *Imam* Al-Husayn b. Masʿud Al-Baghawi said, "This is proof that everything a person does is under His Divine Decree, even laughing and crying. Mujahid and Al-Kalbi said, 'He causes the people of Paradise to laugh and the people of the Hellfire to cry.' Al-Dahhak said, 'He makes the earth laugh with vegetation and the sky cry with rain.' ʿAta b. Abu Muslim said, 'This means He causes happiness and sadness because happiness results in laughter and sadness in tears.'"[3]

Al-Baghawi also mentions Simak b. Harb's narration: He said to Jabir b. Samurah, "Did you sit with the Messenger of Allah?" He said, "Yes, and his companions would gather, recite poetry,

---

[1] Refer to *Lisan Al-Arab* (10/459).
[2] Ibid.
[3] *Tafsir Al-Baghawi* (7/418)

17

and recollect some affairs from the days of *Al-Jahiliyyah*. They would laugh, and the Messenger of Allah would smile."[1]

He concludes with Qatadah's statement, "Someone asked Ibn 'Umar, 'Did the companions of the Messenger of Allah laugh?' He answered, 'Yes, and the *Iman* (faith) in their hearts was greater than a mountain.'"[2]

Yet, no one was more cheerful than the Messenger of Allah ﷺ.

عَنْ عَبْدِ اللهِ بْنِ الْحَارِثِ بْنِ جَزْءٍ، قَالَ: مَا رَأَيْتُ أَحَدًا أَكْثَرَ تَبَسُّمًا مِنْ رَسُولِ اللهِ صَلَّى اللهُ عَلَيْهِ وَسَلَّمَ.

'Abd Allah b. Harith b. Jaz' related, "I saw no one smile more than the Messenger of Allah."[3]

Also, the Prophet's ﷺ smile was his way of laughing.

عَنْ عَبْدِ اللهِ بْنِ الْحَارِثِ بْنِ جَزْءٍ، قَالَ: مَا كَانَ ضَحِكُ رَسُولِ اللهِ صَلَّى اللهُ عَلَيْهِ وَسَلَّمَ إِلاَّ تَبَسُّمًا.

---

[1] Related by Muslim in his *Sahih* (no. 1066). Simak b. Harb asked Jabir b. Samurah: "Did you sit in the company of the Messenger of Allah?" He said, "Yes, very often. He used to sit where he observed the morning prayer till the sun rose. [His companions] would talk about matters [pertaining to the days] of *Jahiliyyah* and laugh [about them] while [the Prophet] merely smiled."

[2] Refer to the *Tafsir* (7/418) of Al-Baghawi.

[3] Related by Al-Tirmidhi in his *Jami'* (no. 2943). It is authenticated by Al-Albani in *Mukhtasar Al-Shama'il Al-Muhammadiyyah* (p. 121).

'Abd Allah b. Harith b. Jaz' stated, "The laughter of Allah's Messenger was simply a smile."[1]

The companions recounted many instances where the Prophet ﷺ laughed:

"What Made You Laugh?"

عَنْ عَلِيِّ بْنِ رَبِيعَةَ، قَالَ: شَهِدْتُ عَلِيًّا، أُتِيَ بِدَابَّةٍ لِيَرْكَبَهَا، فَلَمَّا وَضَعَ رِجْلَهُ فِي الرِّكَابِ، قَالَ: بِسْمِ اللهِ ثَلَاثًا، فَلَمَّا اسْتَوَى عَلَى ظَهْرِهَا، قَالَ: الحَمْدُ لِلَّهِ، ثُمَّ قَالَ: {سُبْحَانَ الَّذِي سَخَّرَ لَنَا هَذَا، وَمَا كُنَّا لَهُ مُقْرِنِينَ وَإِنَّا إِلَى رَبِّنَا لَمُنْقَلِبُونَ}، ثُمَّ قَالَ: الحَمْدُ لِلَّهِ ثَلَاثًا، اللهُ أَكْبَرُ ثَلَاثًا، سُبْحَانَكَ إِنِّي قَدْ ظَلَمْتُ نَفْسِي فَاغْفِرْ لِي، فَإِنَّهُ لَا يَغْفِرُ الذُّنُوبَ إِلاَّ أَنْتَ، ثُمَّ ضَحِكَ. فَقُلْتُ: مِنْ أَيِّ شَيْءٍ ضَحِكْتَ يَا أَمِيرَ الْمُؤْمِنِينَ؟ قَالَ: رَأَيْتُ رَسُولَ اللهِ صَلَّى اللهُ عَلَيْهِ وَسَلَّمَ صَنَعَ كَمَا صَنَعْتُ، ثُمَّ ضَحِكَ، فَقُلْتُ: مِنْ أَيِّ شَيْءٍ ضَحِكْتَ يَا رَسُولَ اللهِ؟ قَالَ: إِنَّ رَبَّكَ لَيَعْجَبُ مِنْ عَبْدِهِ إِذَا قَالَ: رَبِّ اغْفِرْ لِي ذُنُوبِي إِنَّهُ لَا يَغْفِرُ الذُّنُوبَ غَيْرُكَ.

'Ali b. Rabi'ah said, "I was present with 'Ali when someone brought him a riding beast. When he placed his foot in the stirrup, he said, 'In the name of Allah (thrice).' Then, when he sat on its back, he said, 'All praise is for Allah.' He then said,

سُبْحَانَ الَّذِي سَخَّرَ لَنَا هَذَا، وَمَا كُنَّا لَهُ مُقْرِنِينَ وَإِنَّا إِلَى رَبِّنَا لَمُنْقَلِبُونَ

"Glory be to Him Who has made this subservient to us, for we had not the strength, and to our Lord do we return."

---

[1] Related by Al-Tirmidhi in his *Jami'* (no. 2947). It is authenticated by Al-Albani in *Mukhtasar Al-Shama'il Al-Muhammadiyyah* (p. 121).

He said, 'All praise is for Allah (thrice)'; Allah is the Greatest (thrice); glory is to You, I have wronged myself, so forgive me, for only You forgive sins.' He laughed.

'Why did you laugh?' someone asked.

'I saw the Messenger of Allah do the same and laugh. I asked, 'O Messenger of Allah, what made you laugh?'

'Your Lord, Most High, is pleased with His servant when he says, "Forgive me of my sins." [The servant] knows that no one forgives sins except Him,' he said."[1]

---

[1]. This narration is collected by Al-Tirmidi in his *Jami'* (no. 3446). Al-Albani authenticated it in *Sahih Al-Tirmidhi* (no. 3446).

20

"How Did You Know It Was a Ruqya?"

عَنْ أَبِي سَعِيدٍ رَضِيَ اللهُ عَنْهُ قَالَ أَنْطَلَقَ نَفَرٌ مِنْ أَصْحَابِ النَّبِيِّ صَلَّى اللهُ عَلَيْهِ وَسَلَّمَ فِي سَفْرَةٍ سَافَرُوهَا حَتَّى نَزَلُوا عَلَى حَيٍّ مِنْ أَحْيَاءِ الْعَرَبِ فَاسْتَضَافُوهُمْ فَأَبَوْا أَنْ يُضَيِّفُوهُمْ فَلُدِغَ سَيِّدُ ذَلِكَ الْحَيِّ فَسَعَوْا لَهُ بِكُلِّ شَيْءٍ لَا يَنْفَعُهُ شَيْءٌ فَقَالَ بَعْضُهُمْ لَوْ أَتَيْتُمْ هَؤُلَاءِ الرَّهْطَ الَّذِينَ نَزَلُوا لَعَلَّهُ أَنْ يَكُونَ عِنْدَ بَعْضِهِمْ شَيْءٌ فَأَتَوْهُمْ فَقَالُوا يَا أَيُّهَا الرَّهْطُ إِنَّ سَيِّدَنَا لُدِغَ وَسَعَيْنَا لَهُ بِكُلِّ شَيْءٍ لَا يَنْفَعُهُ فَهَلْ عِنْدَ أَحَدٍ مِنْكُمْ مِنْ شَيْءٍ فَقَالَ بَعْضُهُمْ نَعَمْ وَاللهِ إِنِّي لَأَرْقِي وَلَكِنْ وَاللهِ لَقَدِ اسْتَضَفْنَاكُمْ فَلَمْ تُضَيِّفُونَا فَمَا أَنَا بِرَاقٍ لَكُمْ حَتَّى تَجْعَلُوا لَنَا جُعْلًا فَصَالَحُوهُمْ عَلَى قَطِيعٍ مِنَ الْغَنَمِ فَانْطَلَقَ يَتْفِلُ عَلَيْهِ وَيَقْرَأُ الْحَمْدُ لِلَّهِ رَبِّ الْعَالَمِينَ فَكَأَنَّمَا نُشِطَ مِنْ عِقَالٍ فَانْطَلَقَ يَمْشِي وَمَا بِهِ قَلَبَةٌ قَالَ فَأَوْفَوْهُمْ جُعْلَهُمُ الَّذِي صَالَحُوهُمْ عَلَيْهِ فَقَالَ بَعْضُهُمُ اقْسِمُوا فَقَالَ الَّذِي رَقَى لَا تَفْعَلُوا حَتَّى نَأْتِيَ النَّبِيَّ صَلَّى اللهُ عَلَيْهِ وَسَلَّمَ فَنَذْكُرَ لَهُ الَّذِي كَانَ فَنَنْظُرَ مَا يَأْمُرُنَا فَقَدِمُوا عَلَى رَسُولِ اللهِ صَلَّى اللهُ عَلَيْهِ وَسَلَّمَ فَذَكَرُوا لَهُ فَقَالَ وَمَا يُدْرِيكَ أَنَّهَا رُقْيَةٌ ثُمَّ قَالَ قَدْ أَصَبْتُمْ اقْسِمُوا وَاضْرِبُوا لِي مَعَكُمْ سَهْمًا فَضَحِكَ رَسُولُ اللهِ صَلَّى اللهُ عَلَيْهِ وَسَلَّمَ قَالَ أَبُو عَبْدِ اللهِ وَقَالَ شُعْبَةُ حَدَّثَنَا أَبُو بِشْرٍ سَمِعْتُ.

Some of the Prophet's companions journeyed until they reached some Arab tribes. They asked the tribes to host them, but they refused. The chief of that tribe was then bitten by a snake (or stung by a scorpion), and they tried their best to cure him, but in vain. One of them said, "Nothing has benefited him. Will you go to the people who stayed here last night? Perhaps one of them might possess something [as treatment]." They went to the companions and said, "Our chief has been bitten by a snake (or stung by a scorpion), and we have tried everything, but he has not improved. Do you have anything [useful]?" One of them replied, "Yes, by Allah, I can recite a

21

ruqya. But as you have refused to host us, I will not recite it for you unless you compensate us." They agreed to pay them a flock of sheep. The companion then went and recited [*Al-Fatihah*] and puffed[1] over the chief, who became well as if he had been released from restraint. He got up and started walking, showing no signs of sickness. So, they paid them what they agreed upon.

Some of [the companions] then suggested dividing their earnings among themselves. However, the one who performed the recitation said, "Do not divide them until we inform the Prophet ﷺ and await his order." So, they went to Allah's Messenger and told him what happened. Allah's Messenger asked, "How did you know that *Surah Al-Fatihah* was a *ruqya*?"[2] Then he added, "You have done the right thing.[3] Divide [what you have earned] and allot me a share." The Prophet ﷺ then laughed.[4]

The Prophet ﷺ laughed to show his approval and pleasure, demonstrating his warmth and openness towards his companions. Some scholars suggest he did this to comfort them and put their minds at rest.

---

[1] This involves blowing air with a small amount of saliva. Ibn Abu Hamzah said, "Spitting during *ruqya* occurs after the recitation to transfer its blessing to the saliva." Refer to *Fath Al-Bari* (4/456).

[2] Al-Daraqutni's report states, "So I said, O Messenger of Allah, it was something inspired in my heart." This indicates that he did not have prior knowledge of the legitimacy of performing *ruqya* with *Al-Fatihah*. See *Fath Al-Bari* (4/457).

[3] He may have approved of their performing the *ruqya* or their decision to await his permission before dividing up the payment. Allah knows best. Refer to *Fath Al-Bari* (4/457).

[4] Collected by Al-Bukhari in his *Sahih* (no. 2156).

Ibn Hajr said, "It seems [the Prophet] intended to put them at ease, similar to the story of the wild donkey,[1] *et cetera*."[2]

---

[1] He is referring to the narration in the two *Sahihs*: Al-Sa'b b. Jath-thamah Al-Laythi narrated that he presented wild donkey meat to the Prophet while he was in [the area of] Al-Abwa' or Waddan. The Prophet declined it. But when [the Prophet] saw the look on his face, he said to him, "We only declined because we are in the state of *Ihram*." This narration is collected by Al-Bukhari in his *Sahih* (no. 1729) and Muslim in his *Sahih* (no. 1193).
[2] *Fath Al-Bari* (4/457)

"Give Me Something From the Wealth of Allah"

عَنْ أَنَسِ بْنِ مَالِكٍ قَالَ كُنْتُ أَمْشِي مَعَ رَسُولِ اللهِ صَلَّى اللهُ عَلَيْهِ وَسَلَّمَ وَعَلَيْهِ بُرْدٌ
نَجْرَانِيٌّ غَلِيظُ الْحَاشِيَةِ فَأَدْرَكَهُ أَعْرَابِيٌّ فَجَبَذَ بِرِدَائِهِ جَبْذَةً شَدِيدَةً قَالَ أَنَسٌ فَنَظَرْتُ إِلَى
صَفْحَةِ عَاتِقِ النَّبِيِّ صَلَّى اللهُ عَلَيْهِ وَسَلَّمَ وَقَدْ أَثَّرَتْ بِهَا حَاشِيَةُ الرِّدَاءِ مِنْ شِدَّةِ جَبْذَتِهِ
ثُمَّ قَالَ يَا مُحَمَّدُ مُرْ لِي مِنْ مَالِ اللهِ الَّذِي عِنْدَكَ فَالْتَفَتَ إِلَيْهِ فَضَحِكَ ثُمَّ أَمَرَ لَهُ
بِعَطَاءٍ.

Anas b. Malik reported, "I was walking with the Prophet, who was wearing a thick *Najrani* cloak. A Bedouin approached him, grabbed the Prophet's cloak by its hem, and pulled it harshly. I looked at the Prophet's shoulder and saw that the cloak's hem had left a mark on his skin from the force of the pull. Then, the Bedouin said, 'O Muhammad, give me something you possess from Allah's wealth.' The Prophet turned to him, laughed, and then ordered that he be given something."[1]

Ibn Hajr said, "This narration shows the Prophet's forbearance, patience, and ability to overlook harm for the sake of Islam. It also sets a beautiful example for the leaders who come after him in forgiveness, pardoning, and responding with goodness."[2]

---

[1] Collected by Al-Bukhari in his *Sahih* (no. 5738).
[2] *Fath Al-Bari* (10/521)

"Ask Allah to Make Me One of Them"

عَنْ عُبَيْدِ اللهِ بْنِ عَبْدِ الرَّحْمَنِ الْأَنْصَارِيِّ قَالَ سَمِعْتُ أَنَسًا رَضِيَ اللهُ عَنْهُ يَقُولُ دَخَلَ رَسُولُ اللهِ صَلَّى اللهُ عَلَيْهِ وَسَلَّمَ عَلَى ابْنَةِ مِلْحَانَ فَاتَّكَأَ عِنْدَهَا ثُمَّ ضَحِكَ فَقَالَتْ لِمَ تَضْحَكُ يَا رَسُولَ اللهِ فَقَالَ نَاسٌ مِنْ أُمَّتِي يَرْكَبُونَ الْبَحْرَ الْأَخْضَرَ فِي سَبِيلِ اللهِ مَثَلُهُمْ مَثَلُ الْمُلُوكِ عَلَى الْأَسِرَّةِ فَقَالَتْ يَا رَسُولَ اللهِ ذْعُ اللهَ أَنْ يَجْعَلَنِي مِنْهُمْ قَالَ اللَّهُمَّ اجْعَلْهَا مِنْهُمْ ثُمَّ عَادَ فَضَحِكَ فَقَالَتْ لَهُ مِثْلَ أَوْ مِمَّ ذَلِكَ فَقَالَ لَهَا مِثْلَ ذَلِكَ فَقَالَتْ ذْعُ اللهَ أَنْ يَجْعَلَنِي مِنْهُمْ قَالَ أَنْتِ مِنَ الْأُولِينَ وَلَسْتِ مِنَ الْآخِرِينَ قَالَ أَنَسٌ فَتَزَوَّجَتْ عُبَادَةَ بْنَ الصَّامِتِ فَرَكِبَتْ الْبَحْرَ مَعَ بِنْتِ قَرَظَةَ فَلَمَّا قَفَلَتْ رَكِبَتْ دَابَّتَهَا فَوَقَصَتْ بِهَا فَسَقَطَتْ عَنْهَا فَمَاتَتْ

'Abd Allah b. 'Abd Al-Rahman Al-Ansari said, "I heard Anas b. Malik say, 'The Messenger of Allah entered the house of [Umm Haram] bint Milhan and leaned against something. He then laughed. She said, 'Why do you laugh, O Messenger of Allah?' He said, 'I see some people from my *Ummah* riding the green sea in the way of Allah. They resemble kings upon thrones.' She said, 'O Messenger of Allah, ask Allah to make me one of them.' He said, 'O Allah, make her one of them.'

He laughed again. She said something similar to what she said before, and he said the same thing to her. She said, 'Ask Allah to make me one of them.' He said, 'You are among the first, but you are not among the last.'"

Anas said, "So, she married 'Ubadah b. Al-Samit and rode the sea with the daughter of Qarazah. When she returned, she rode her mount, which stumbled, and she fell from it and died."[1]

Al-Muhaddith Muhammad b. 'Ali Al-Ithyubi said, "This narration clarifies the permissibility of displaying joy when blessings occur and laughing when one is happy. It is based on the Prophet ﷺ laughing delightfully at what he saw [in the dream]."[2]

---

[1] Collected by Al-Bukhari in his *Sahih* (no. 2722) and Muslim in his *Sahih* (no. 1912).
[2] *Al-Bahr Al-Muhit* (32/682)

"We Are Drowning"

عَنْ أَنَسٍ رَضِيَ اللَّهُ عَنْهُ أَنَّ رَجُلًا جَاءَ إِلَى النَّبِيِّ صَلَّى اللَّهُ عَلَيْهِ وَسَلَّمَ يَوْمَ الْجُمُعَةِ وَهُوَ يَخْطُبُ بِالْمَدِينَةِ فَقَالَ قَحَطَ الْمَطَرُ فَاسْتَسْقِ رَبَّكَ فَنَظَرَ إِلَى السَّمَاءِ وَمَا نَرَى مِنْ سَحَابٍ فَاسْتَسْقَى فَنَشَأَ السَّحَابُ بَعْضُهُ إِلَى بَعْضٍ ثُمَّ مُطِرُوا حَتَّى سَالَتْ مَثَاعِبُ الْمَدِينَةِ فَمَا زَالَتْ إِلَى الْجُمُعَةِ الْمُقْبِلَةِ مَا تُقْلِعُ ثُمَّ قَامَ ذَلِكَ الرَّجُلُ أَوْ غَيْرُهُ وَالنَّبِيُّ صَلَّى اللَّهُ عَلَيْهِ وَسَلَّمَ يَخْطُبُ فَقَالَ غَرِقْنَا فَادْعُ رَبَّكَ يَحْبِسْهَا عَنَّا فَضَحِكَ ثُمَّ قَالَ اللَّهُمَّ حَوَالَيْنَا وَلَا عَلَيْنَا مَرَّتَيْنِ أَوْ ثَلَاثًا فَجَعَلَ السَّحَابُ يَتَصَدَّعُ عَنِ الْمَدِينَةِ يَمِينًا وَشِمَالًا يُمْطَرُ مَا حَوَالَيْنَا وَلَا يُمْطِرُ مِنْهَا شَيْءٌ مُرِيهِمْ اللَّهُ كَرَامَةَ نَبِيِّهِ صَلَّى اللَّهُ عَلَيْهِ وَسَلَّمَ وَإِجَابَةَ دَعْوَتِهِ.

Anas reported that a man came to the Prophet on a Friday while he was delivering a sermon in Al-Madinah. The man said, "Drought has afflicted us, so seek rain from your Lord." The Prophet looked at the sky and saw no clouds, so he sought rain. Clouds gathered, and rain poured until the following Friday. The man or someone else stood up while the Prophet delivered a sermon and said, "We are drowning, so pray to your Lord to hold it back from us." The Prophet laughed and said, "O Allah, around us and not on us," two or three times. The clouds then moved away from Al-Madinah, raining around it but not on it, showing them the honor of His Prophet and the acceptance of his supplication.[1]

Ibn Hajr said, "The ninth narration is the *hadith* of Anas about the one who requested rain and then sought its cessation,

---

[1] Collected by Al-Bukhari in his *Sahih* (no. 5742).

highlighting the Prophet's  laughter when the man said, 'We are drowning.'"[1]

───── ✦ ─────

[1] *Fath Al-Bari* (10/522)

"You Have Limited Something Vast"

عَنْ أَبِي هُرَيْرَةَ قَالَ دَخَلَ أَعْرَابِيٌّ الْمَسْجِدَ وَرَسُولُ اللهِ صَلَّى اللهُ عَلَيْهِ وَسَلَّمَ جَالِسٌ
فَقَالَ اللَّهُمَّ اغْفِرْ لِي وَلِمُحَمَّدٍ وَلَا تَغْفِرْ لِأَحَدٍ مَعَنَا فَضَحِكَ رَسُولُ اللهِ صَلَّى اللهُ عَلَيْهِ
وَسَلَّمَ وَقَالَ لَقَدْ اخْتَطَرْتَ وَاسِعًا ثُمَّ وَلَّى حَتَّى إِذَا كَانَ فِي نَاحِيَةِ الْمَسْجِدِ فَشَجَ يَبُولُ
فَقَالَ الْأَعْرَابِيُّ بَعْدَ أَنْ فَقِهَ فَقَامَ إِلَيَّ بِأَبِي وَأُمِّي فَلَمْ يُؤَنِّبْ وَلَمْ يَسُبَّ فَقَالَ إِنَّ هَذَا
الْمَسْجِدَ لَا يُبَالُ فِيهِ وَإِنَّمَا بُنِيَ لِذِكْرِ اللهِ وَللصَّلَاةِ ثُمَّ أَمَرَ بِسَجْلٍ مِنْ مَاءٍ فَأُوقِعَ عَلَى
بَوْلِهِ.

Abu Hurayrah reported that a Bedouin entered the mosque
when the Messenger of Allah was sitting there. [The man] said,
"O Allah, forgive me and Muhammad, and do not forgive
anyone else." The Messenger of Allah laughed, saying, "You
have limited something vast." Then the Bedouin turned away,
went to a corner of the mosque, spread his legs, and urinated.
After better understanding, the Bedouin said, "He got up and
came to me, and may my father and mother be ransomed for
him. He did not rebuke me nor revile me." He said, "This
mosque is not for urinating in. Rather, it is built for the
remembrance of Allah and prayer." Then, he called for a large
vessel of water and poured it over the place where he had
urinated.[1]

Al-Sindi said, "In other words, you have asked to prevent
something or someone from receiving Allah's mercy and
forgiveness, though it cannot possibly be withheld."[2]

---

[1] Collected by Ibn Majah in his *Sunan* (no. 529) and authenticated by Al-
Albani in *Sahih Sunan Ibn Majah* (no. 529).
[2] *Hashiyah Al-Sindi ala Sunan Ibn Majah* (1/189)

Additionally, some companions made the Messenger of Allah ﷺ laugh:

"Do Not Curse Him"

عَنْ عُمَرَ بْنِ الْخَطَّابِ، أَنَّ رَجُلًا عَلَى عَهْدِ النَّبِيِّ صَلَّى اللهُ عَلَيْهِ وَسَلَّمَ كَانَ اسْمُهُ عَبْدَ اللهِ، وَكَانَ يُلَقَّبُ حِمَارًا، وَكَانَ يُضْحِكُ رَسُولَ اللهِ صَلَّى اللهُ عَلَيْهِ وَسَلَّمَ، وَكَانَ النَّبِيُّ صَلَّى اللهُ عَلَيْهِ وَسَلَّمَ قَدْ جَلَدَهُ فِي الشَّرَابِ، فَأُتِيَ بِهِ يَوْمًا فَأَمَرَ بِهِ فَجُلِدَ، فَقَالَ رَجُلٌ مِنَ الْقَوْمِ: اللَّهُمَّ الْعَنْهُ، مَا أَكْثَرَ مَا يُؤْتَى بِهِ؟ فَقَالَ النَّبِيُّ صَلَّى اللهُ عَلَيْهِ وَسَلَّمَ: «لَا تَلْعَنُوهُ، فَوَاللهِ مَا عَلِمْتُ إِنَّهُ يُحِبُّ اللهَ وَرَسُولَهُ»

'Umar b. Al-Khattab stated, "During the Prophet's lifetime, a man named 'Abd Allah, nicknamed *Himar* (donkey), used to make Allah's Messenger laugh. The Prophet would lash him for drinking [intoxicants]. One day, he was brought to the Prophet for the same offense and lashed again. Someone said, 'O Allah, curse him! How often has he done this!' The Prophet said, 'Do not curse him, for by Allah, I know he loves Allah and His Messenger.'"[1]

Ibn Hajr mentions that 'Abd Allah used to do things to amuse the Prophet ﷺ. He then cited a narration that a man nicknamed *Himar* sent a gift of honey or fat to Allah's Messenger ﷺ. When the seller came to collect the price, [*Himar*] took him to the Messenger of Allah ﷺ to pay for it. This made the Prophet ﷺ laugh. He then told someone to pay the merchant.[2]

---

[1] Collected by Al-Bukhari in his *Sahih* (no. 6398).
[2] Refer to *Fath Al-Bari* (12/77).

Likewise, we find examples of the noble companions laughing:

"Then She Laughed"

عَنْ عَائِشَةَ: قَالَتْ: إِنْ كَانَ رَسُولُ اللَّهِ لَيُقَبِّلُ بَعْضَ أَزْوَاجِهِ وَهُوَ صَائِمٌ، ثُمَّ ضَحِكَتْ.

'Aishah said, "The Messenger of Allah used to kiss some of his wives while fasting." She then laughed.[1]

Ibn Hajr said, "[The statement], 'She then laughed,' could be interpreted as her laughing in surprise at someone disagreeing with this. Perhaps she was surprised at herself for talking about such a thing, which women are embarrassed to say to men. However, she was compelled by the necessity of conveying knowledge to mention it. The laughter could also be out of shyness for talking about herself in this way or to indicate that she was the subject of the story, making it more credible. Perhaps it was out of joy at her position with the Prophet and his love for her."[2]

---

[1] Collected by Al-Bukhari in his *Sahih* (no. 1928).
[2] *Fath Al-Bari* (4/152)

"How Else Does the Child Resemble His Mother?"

عَنْ أُمِّ سَلَمَةَ أَنَّ أُمَّ سُلَيْمٍ قَالَتْ يَا رَسُولَ اللَّهِ إِنَّ اللَّهَ لَا يَسْتَحِي مِنْ الْحَقِّ هَلْ عَلَى الْمَرْأَةِ غُسْلٌ إِذَا احْتَلَمَتْ قَالَ نَعَمْ إِذَا رَأَتْ الْمَاءَ فَضَحِكَتْ أُمُّ سَلَمَةَ فَقَالَتْ أَتَحْتَلِمُ الْمَرْأَةُ فَقَالَ النَّبِيُّ صَلَّى اللَّهُ عَلَيْهِ وَسَلَّمَ فَبِمَ شَبَهُ الْوَلَدِ.

Umm Salamah reported that Umm Sulaym said, "O Messenger of Allah, Allah does not shy away from the truth. Is there a *ghusl* (ritual bath) for a woman if she has a wet dream?" He said, "Yes, if she sees discharge." Umm Salamah laughed and said, "Does a woman have discharge?" The Prophet said, "How else does the child resemble [his mother]?"[1]

Ibn Hajr said, "Umm Salamah laughed because the discussion was in the presence of the Prophet ﷺ. Also, he did not object to her laughter. Rather, he objected to her dismissing the possibility of women having wet dreams."[2]

---

[1] Collected by Al-Bukhari in his *Sahih* (no. 5740).
[2] *Fath Al-Bari* (10/522)

Affirming Allah's Laughter

The people of *Sunnah* affirm for Allah what He affirms for Himself, including the attribute of laughter. This is established in the Revelation:

عَنْ أَبِي رَزِينٍ قَالَ: قَالَ رَسُولُ اللهِ صَلَّى اللهُ عَلَيْهِ وَسَلَّمَ ضَحِكَ رَبُّنَا مِنْ قُنُوطِ عِبَادِهِ وَقُرْبِ غِيَرِهِ قَالَ قُلْتُ يَا رَسُولَ اللهِ أَوَ يَضْحَكُ الرَّبُّ قَالَ نَعَمْ قُلْتُ لَنْ نَعْدَمَ مِنْ رَبٍّ يَضْحَكُ خَيْرًا.

Abu Razin reported that the Messenger of Allah ﷺ said, "Our Lord laughs at the despair of His servants, and He soon changes it for them."

"O Messenger of Allah, does the Lord laugh?" I said.

"Yes," he said.

"We will never lack good from a Lord who laughs," I said.[1]

This is also established in the *hadith* of Abu Hurayrah:

عَنْ أَبِي هُرَيْرَةَ أَنَّ رَسُولَ اللهِ صَلَّى اللهُ عَلَيْهِ وَسَلَّمَ قَالَ يَضْحَكُ اللهُ إِلَى رَجُلَيْنِ يَقْتُلُ أَحَدُهُمَا الْآخَرَ كِلَاهُمَا يَدْخُلُ الْجَنَّةَ فَقَالُوا كَيْفَ يَا رَسُولَ اللهِ قَالَ يُقَاتِلُ هَذَا فِي سَبِيلِ اللهِ عَزَّ وَجَلَّ فَيُسْتَشْهَدُ ثُمَّ يَتُوبُ اللهُ عَلَى الْقَاتِلِ فَيُسْلِمُ فَيُقَاتِلُ فِي سَبِيلِ اللهِ عَزَّ وَجَلَّ فَيُسْتَشْهَدُ.

---

[1] Collected by Ibn Majah in his *Sunan* (no. 181) and authenticated by Al-Albani in *Sahih Sunan Ibn Majah* (no. 181).

Note: Ibn Majah includes this narration in *Kitab al-Muqaddimah* (Introduction) under "The Chapter on What the Jahmiyyah Denied," which addresses their denial of Allah's attributes, including laughter.

Abu Hurayrah reported that the Messenger of Allah said, "Allah laughs at two men. One of them killed the other, yet they both entered Paradise." The companions asked, "How is that, O Messenger of Allah?" He said, "This one fought in the way of Allah and was martyred, then his killer repented, embracing Islam, and was also martyred."[1]

Concerning this, *Al-Allamah* Muhammad b. Salih Al-'Uthaymin said, "This affirms [the attribute of] laughter for Allah, glorified and exalted is He. It is true laughter, but it does not resemble that of the creation. It is a laughter befitting His majesty and greatness, and we cannot perceive it. We cannot say that Allah has a mouth, teeth, or anything similar, but we affirm laughter for Allah in a manner that befits His majesty."[2]

Also, in his *Kitab Al-Tawhid*, Ibn Khuzaymah names one chapter: "The affirmation of our Lord's laughter, the Mighty and Majestic, without describing it with a quality. His laughter is not likened to that of the creation, nor is their laughter like His. Rather, we believe He laughs, as the Prophet ﷺ informed us. We remain silent about the quality of His laughter, as Allah, the Mighty and Majestic, has kept the knowledge of it to Himself. We accept the Prophet's teachings wholeheartedly and do not speak about what Allah has not revealed."[3]

Finally, Al-Ajurri said, "Chapter on the Belief That Allah Almighty Laughs: Know—may Allah guide us and you to the

---

[1] Collected by Muslim in his *Sahih* (no. 1890).

[2] *Sharh Al-Aqidah Al-Wasitiyyah* (2/24)

[3] *Al-Tawhid* (2/563)

path of righteousness in speech and deed—that the people of truth describe Allah Almighty with what He, His Messenger ﷺ, and the companions, may Allah be pleased with them, have described Him. This is the way of the scholars who followed [right guidance] and did not innovate. One does not ask 'how' concerning [His Laughter]. Rather, one submits to Him and believes that Allah laughs. This was narrated by the Prophet ﷺ and his companions—may Allah be pleased with them. No one denies this except one who is blameworthy with the people of truth."[1]

---

[1] *Al-Sharīʿah* (p. 277)

Joking in the Islamic Legislation

Joking involves using humor light-heartedly[1] to amuse others and provoke laughter through remarks or actions.

Muhammad b. Muhammad Al-Zabidi states that "joking means bringing joy to others through kindness and understanding, without causing harm. Mockery and ridicule are excluded [from this]. The *Imams* have said that being excessively playful undermines a person's honor and dignity. However, completely avoiding humor goes against the Prophet's traditions, which we must follow. The best approach lies in moderation."[2]

The Prophet ﷺ perfectly captured this definition:

عَنْ أَبِي هُرَيْرَةَ: قَالَ: قَالَ رَسُولُ اللهِ صَلَّى اللهُ عَلَيْهِ وَسَلَّمَ: يَا أَبَا هُرَيْرَةَ كُنْ وَرِعًا، أَشْكَرَ النَّاسِ، وَأَحِبَّ لِلنَّاسِ مَا تُحِبُّ لِنَفْسِكَ، تَكُنْ أَعْبَدَ النَّاسِ، وَكُنْ قَنِعًا، تَكُنْ تَكُنْ مُؤْمِنًا، وَأَحْسِنْ جِوَارَ مَنْ جَاوَرَكَ، تَكُنْ مُسْلِمًا، وَأَقِلَّ الضَّحِكَ، فَإِنَّ كَثْرَةَ الضَّحِكِ تُمِيتُ الْقَلْبَ.

Abu Hurayrah related that the Messenger of Allah ﷺ said, "O Abu Hurayrah! Be dutiful in worship, and you will be the most devout person. Be content, and you will be the most thankful person. Love for others what you love for yourself, and you will be a believer. Be good to your

---

[1] Refer to *Lisan Al-Arab* (2/593).
[2] Refer to *Taj Al-'Urus min Jawahir Al-Qamus* (2/322).

nearest neighbors, and you will be a Muslim. Laugh moderately, for excessive laughter deadens the heart."[1]

A similar wording further clarifies this:

عَنِ الْحَسَنِ، عَنْ أَبِي هُرَيْرَةَ، قَالَ: قَالَ رَسُولُ اللهِ صَلَّى اللهُ عَلَيْهِ وَسَلَّمَ: مَنْ يَأْخُذُ عَنِّي هَؤُلَاءِ الْكَلِمَاتِ فَيَعْمَلُ بِهِنَّ أَوْ يُعَلِّمُ مَنْ يَعْمَلُ بِهِنَّ؟ فَقَالَ أَبُو هُرَيْرَةَ: فَقُلْتُ: أَنَا يَا رَسُولَ اللهِ، فَأَخَذَ بِيَدِي فَعَدَّ خَمْسًا وَقَالَ: اتَّقِ الْمَحَارِمَ تَكُنْ أَعْبَدَ النَّاسِ، وَارْضَ بِمَا قَسَمَ اللهُ لَكَ تَكُنْ أَغْنَى النَّاسِ، وَأَحْسِنْ إِلَى جَارِكَ تَكُنْ مُؤْمِنًا، وَأَحِبَّ لِلنَّاسِ مَا تُحِبُّ لِنَفْسِكَ تَكُنْ مُسْلِمًا، وَلَا تُكْثِرِ الضَّحِكَ، فَإِنَّ كَثْرَةَ الضَّحِكِ تُمِيتُ الْقَلْبَ.

Abu Hurayrah reported that the Messenger of Allah ﷺ said, "Whoever receives these words from me, let him act on them or convey them to someone who will."

"I will, O Messenger of Allah!" I said. So, he took me by the hand and named five things. He said, "Avoid the impermissible, and you will be the most devout person. Be content with whatever Allah has given you, and you will be the richest person. Be good to your neighbor, and you will be a believer. Love for others what you love for yourself, and you will be a Muslim. Do not laugh excessively, for excessive laughter deadens the heart."[2]

---

[1] Related by Ibn Majah in his *Sunan* (no. 4193). It has been authenticated by Al-Albani in his *Silsilah Al-Ahadith Al-Sahihah* (no. 506).
[2] Related by Al-Tirmidhi in his *Jami'* (no. 2305) upon the authority of Abu Hurayrah. It has been graded *Hasan* by Al-Albani in *Sahih Al-Tirmidhi* (no. 2304).

Concerning this, *Al-Muhaddith* Muhammad b. 'Abd Al-Rahman Al-Mubarakfuri said, "This means it leaves the heart in total darkness like the dead, unable to seek solace or shield itself from harm. This narration is from the concise yet comprehensive words [of Allah's Messenger]."[1]

Also, *Al-Imam* 'Abd Al-Ra'uf Al-Manawi said, "Excessive laughter hardens the heart. This leads to heedlessness, which kills the heart [...] it can divert one's attention from important matters... It diminishes one's dignity, undermines one's ability to command respect, and hinders one from being seen as having meaningful thoughts or worth... Excessive laughter and attachment to worldly affairs are lethal poisons that flow through one's veins. They strip away the fear of Allah's punishment, the sadness over one's sins, the remembrance of death, and the apprehension of the Day of Resurrection. Thus, the heart succumbs to spiritual death.

﴿وَفَرِحُواْ بِٱلْحَيَوٰةِ ٱلدُّنْيَا وَمَا ٱلْحَيَوٰةُ ٱلدُّنْيَا فِى ٱلْآخِرَةِ إِلَّا مَتَٰعٌ﴾

> 'And they rejoice over the life of this world, yet the life of this world with respect to the afterlife is nothing but temporary, paltry amusement.'"
>
> [*Al-Ra'd* 13:26][2]

He also stated, "Laughter harms the heart when we rejoice in this worldly life and take pride in this joy. The heart has both spiritual life and death. Its life comes from continuous

---

[1] Refer to *Tuhfah Al-Ahwadhi* (6/487).
[2] Refer to *Fayd Al-Qadir* (3/76).

obedience, while its death comes from heeding the call of anything other than Allah, like our ego, stubborn desires, or *Shaytan*."[1]

Imam Yahya b. Sharaf Al-Nawawi said, "Excessive joking is forbidden, for it leads to excessive laughter, which hardens the heart and diverts one from the remembrance of Allah. It often results in harm, malice, and a loss of dignity and honor. However, if joking is free from these affairs, it falls under permissible joking, in which the Messenger of Allah ﷺ would engage."[2]

Sufyan Al-Thawri was asked, "Is joking considered a shortcoming?" He replied, "No. Rather, it is from the *Sunnah*. However, one should do it appropriately and put it in its proper context."[3]

One can also see this from the Prophet's companions.

عَنْ بَكْرِ بْنِ عَبْدِ اللهِ قَالَ: كَانَ أَصْحَابُ النَّبِيِّ صَلَّى اللهُ عَلَيْهِ وَسَلَّمَ، يَتَبَادَحُونَ بِالْبَطِّيخِ، فَإِذَا كَانَتِ الْحَقَائِقُ كَانُوا هُمُ الرِّجَالُ.

Bakr b. 'Abd Allah said, "The Prophet's companions used to [play by] throwing watermelon rinds at each other, but when it was time for seriousness, they were [real] men."[4]

---

[1] Ibid., 5/52.
[2] Refer to *Al-Adhkar* (p. 864) of Al-Nawawi.
[3] Refer to *Sharh Al-Sunnah* (31/381) of Al-Baghawi.
[4] Related by Al-Bukhari in his *Al-Adab Al-Mufrad* (no. 266). It has been authenticated by Al-Albani in *Silsilah Al-Ahadith Al-Sahihah* (no. 435).

According to the narrations above, joking is allowed in Islamic legislation as long as it avoids mockery and ridicule. Additionally, it should be done in moderation because excessive joking and laughter can numb the heart. This is best understood through the words of the Prophet ﷺ to his companion Hanzalah:

عَنْ حَنْظَلَةَ الْأُسَيِّدِيِّ، قَالَ: - وَكَانَ مِنْ كُتَّابِ رَسُولِ اللهِ صَلَّى اللهُ عَلَيْهِ وَسَلَّمَ - قَالَ: لَقِيَنِي أَبُو بَكْرٍ، فَقَالَ: كَيْفَ أَنْتَ؟ فَقَالَ: يَا حَنْظَلَةُ قَالَ: قُلْتُ: نَافَقَ حَنْظَلَةُ، قَالَ: سُبْحَانَ اللهِ مَا تَقُولُ؟ قَالَ: قُلْتُ: نَكُونُ عِنْدَ رَسُولِ اللهِ صَلَّى اللهُ عَلَيْهِ وَسَلَّمَ، يُذَكِّرُنَا بِالنَّارِ وَالْجَنَّةِ، حَتَّى كَأَنَّا رَأْيُ عَيْنٍ، فَإِذَا خَرَجْنَا مِنْ عِنْدِ رَسُولِ اللهِ صَلَّى اللهُ عَلَيْهِ وَسَلَّمَ، عَافَسْنَا الْأَزْوَاجَ وَالْأَوْلَادَ وَالضَّيْعَاتِ، فَنَسِينَا كَثِيرًا، قَالَ أَبُو بَكْرٍ: فَوَاللهِ إِنَّا لَنَلْقَى مِثْلَ هَذَا، فَانْطَلَقْتُ أَنَا وَأَبُو بَكْرٍ، حَتَّى دَخَلْنَا عَلَى رَسُولِ اللهِ صَلَّى اللهُ عَلَيْهِ وَسَلَّمَ، قُلْتُ: نَافَقَ حَنْظَلَةُ، يَا رَسُولَ اللهِ فَقَالَ رَسُولُ اللهِ صَلَّى اللهُ عَلَيْهِ وَسَلَّمَ «وَمَا ذَاكَ؟» قُلْتُ: يَا رَسُولَ اللهِ نَكُونُ عِنْدَكَ، تُذَكِّرُنَا بِالنَّارِ وَالْجَنَّةِ، حَتَّى كَأَنَّا رَأْيُ عَيْنٍ، فَإِذَا خَرَجْنَا مِنْ عِنْدِكَ، عَافَسْنَا الْأَزْوَاجَ وَالْأَوْلَادَ وَالضَّيْعَاتِ، نَسِينَا كَثِيرًا فَقَالَ رَسُولُ اللهِ صَلَّى اللهُ عَلَيْهِ وَسَلَّمَ: «وَالَّذِي نَفْسِي بِيَدِهِ إِنْ لَوْ تَدُومُونَ عَلَى مَا تَكُونُونَ عِنْدِي، وَفِي الذِّكْرِ، لَصَافَحَتْكُمُ الْمَلَائِكَةُ عَلَى فُرُشِكُمْ وَفِي طُرُقِكُمْ، وَلَكِنْ يَا حَنْظَلَةُ سَاعَةً وَسَاعَةً» ثَلَاثَ مَرَّاتٍ

The noble companion Hanzalah Al-Usayyidi, a scribe of Allah's Messenger, stated, "Abu Bakr met me and said, 'How are you, O Hanzalah?'

'Hanzalah is a hypocrite,' I said.

'Allah is free from all imperfection. What are you saying?'

40

'When we are with the Messenger of Allah, he reminds us of the Hellfire and the Paradise until it is as if we can see them with our very eyes, but when we leave from him and go[1] to our families and children, we forget much [of what the Messenger of Allah told us].'

'By Allah, the same happens to us,' Abu Bakr said.

So, Abu Bakr and I went to the Messenger of Allah, and I said, 'O Messenger of Allah, Hanzalah is a hypocrite.'

'How is that?' he said.

'O Messenger of Allah, when we are with you, you remind us of the Hellfire and Paradise until it is as if we can see it before our very eyes, but then when we leave you and go to our families and children, we forget much [of what you told us],' I said.

'By the One in Whose Hand is my soul, if you could maintain the state of remembrance that you experience when you are with me, the angels would greet you in your homes and on the streets. However, O Hanzalah, there is a time for [remembrance] and a time for [laughter and amusement].'"[2]

---

[1] In another wording, he states, "...I laugh with my children and play with my wife..." Refer to *Sahih Muslim* (no. 4916).
[2] Related by Muslim in his *Sahih* (no. 2750).

"Isa Had No Father"

'Abd Al-Rahman Al-Mubarakfuri clarified that· Al-Tirmidhi, whose given name was Muhammad, preferred his *kunyah* Abu 'Isa. Scholars debate using "Abu 'Isa" based on narrations in Ibn Abu Shaybah's *Al-Musannaf*, particularly in the chapter "Disapproval of the *Kunyah* Abu Isa."

It is reported that the Prophet ﷺ objected to a man using Abu 'Isa, saying, "Isa had no father." Likewise, 'Umar b. Khattab reprimanded one of his sons for taking the *kunyah*, stating, "Isa had no father."

Some scholars state that the first *hadith* (i.e., the Prophet's objection) is *mursal*[1], and the second one (i.e., 'Umar's reprimand) is *mawquf*[2]. Even if the *hadith* attributed to the Prophet ﷺ were authentic, it does not explicitly prohibit using the *kunyah* "Abu 'Isa." This is merely the Prophet ﷺ humorously remarking that 'Isa had no father, akin to his response to a companion requesting a riding animal, where he jokingly mentioned providing him with a she-camel's calf. The Prophet ﷺ said, 'I will give you the *naqah's* (she-camel's) calf [to ride].' He replied, 'O Messenger of Allah, what will I do with a calf?' Al-Tirmidhi includes this narration in the chapter on the Prophet's joking (*Al-Mizah*).[3]

---

[1] A *mursal hadith* is when a *tabi'i* directly reports a statement or action of the Prophet without mentioning an intermediary companion.

[2] A *mawquf hadith* is when a chain of transmission stops at a companion, rather than extending to the Messenger of Allah ﷺ.

[3] Refer to *The Introduction to Tuhfah Al-Ahwadhi* (pp. 238-239).

Section Two: Prohibited Joking: The Impermissibility of Joking Concerning Affairs of Religion and the Signs of Allah

Based on the conditions mentioned by the *Imams* Al-Manawi and Al-Nawawi, et al., let us explore some instances where joking is impermissible. We start with the most severe prohibition: joking about religious matters. This act completely removes a person from the faith, as indicated by Allah's statement:

﴿ وَلَئِن سَأَلۡتَهُمۡ لَيَقُولُنَّ إِنَّمَا كُنَّا نَخُوضُ وَنَلۡعَبُ ۚ قُلۡ أَبِٱللَّهِ وَءَايَٰتِهِۦ وَرَسُولِهِۦ كُنتُمۡ تَسۡتَهۡزِءُونَ ٦٥ لَا تَعۡتَذِرُواْ قَدۡ كَفَرۡتُم بَعۡدَ إِيمَٰنِكُمۡ ۚ إِن نَّعۡفُ عَن طَآئِفَةٖ مِّنكُمۡ نُعَذِّبۡ طَآئِفَةَۢ بِأَنَّهُمۡ كَانُواْ مُجۡرِمِينَ ٦٦ ﴾

"And if you ask them (O Muhammad), they will say: We did but talk and jest. Say: Was it at Allah and His Revelations and His Messenger that you were mocking? Make no excuse. You have disbelieved after you confessed belief. If We forgive a party of you, a party of you We shall punish because they have been guilty."

[*Al-Tawbah* 9:65-66]

Commenting on these verses, *Shaykh* ʿAbd Al-Rahman b. Nasir Al-Saʿdi notes, "A group of them defamed the Muslims and their religion during the Tabuk expedition, saying, 'We have seen nothing like our reciters (i.e., the Prophet ﷺ and his companions). They have the most insatiable appetites, deceitful tongues, and cowardly [hearts] in

43

battle.' However, when they heard the Prophet ﷺ had learned about their remarks, they approached him with excuses, claiming, 'We were only running our mouths and jesting,' implying that they had no intention of defaming or slandering anyone.

Allah clarified their falsehood and deception, saying, 'Say: Was it Allah, His Revelations, and His Messenger that you were mocking? Do not make excuses. You have disbelieved after your belief.' Mocking Allah, His Signs, and His Messenger is an act of disbelief, which removes one from the religion. The foundation of the faith is based on honoring and respecting Allah, His Religion, and His Messenger ﷺ. Mockery of any of these is incompatible with and contradictory to that foundation [...] Anyone who mocks or belittles anything from the Book of Allah or the authentic *Sunnah*, or mocks and belittles Allah's Messenger ﷺ, has indeed disbelieved in Allah. However, it is essential to note that repentance is accepted for every sin, regardless of its magnitude."[1]

Shaykh Muhammad b. Salih Al-'Uthaymin said, "Divine Lordship, Prophethood, Revelation, and Religion are sacred matters that must be honored. It is impermissible for anyone to show disrespect towards them, whether by mocking them to make others laugh or to make fun of them. Engaging in such actions indicates one's disbelief, as it demonstrates disrespect towards Allah, His Messengers, His Books, and His Laws. Whoever does this must repent to Allah for his actions, as that is a kind of hypocrisy. So, he must repent to Allah, seek His

---

[1] Refer to *Taysir Al-Karim Al-Rahman* (p. 343).

forgiveness, mend his ways, develop fear of Allah, and show reverence towards Him and love for Him in his heart. And Allah is the source of strength."[1] [2]

---

[1] Refer to *Al-Majmu Al-Thamin* (1/63) of Muhammad b. Salih Al-'Uthaymin.

[2] Let this be a reminder to those who produce and spread shameful, irreverent memes and skits on social media platforms like Instagram, TikTok, and Snapchat, satirizing matters of religion: legislated dress, plural marriage (a favorite target of their darts and arrows), *et cetera*. Even our beloved Prophet ﷺ and his noble family are not safe from their depraved minds. Moreover, we find some "men" with little concern for the threat of Allah's punishment, wearing women's clothes and imitating their mannerisms in these skits. Are they unaware that Allah's Messenger "cursed men who imitate women"? Perhaps they are more concerned about the creation's laughter than the Creator's anger.

Joking in Divorce

In Islam, certain matters are taken seriously, even if said in jest. Divorce is one of them. *Shaykh* Salih Al-Fawzan was asked about a man jokingly saying to his wife, "You are divorced."

He responded, "There is no room for humor in such things. Even if one says it in jest, it is taken seriously, as stated by the Messenger of Allah.[1] So, if someone says, 'You are divorced,' even jokingly, the divorce is valid."[2]

Also, *Shaykh* Ibn Baz said, "Divorce should not be taken lightly or played with, for it is a matter of religion. A Muslim must be certain and should only pronounce a divorce after reflecting and making a firm decision. If the need arises, divorce is permissible, but it should not be taken lightly."[3]

---

[1] He is referring to Abu Hurayrah's report that the Prophet ﷺ said, "There are three things which, whether undertaken seriously or in jest, are treated as serious: marriage, divorce, and taking back a wife [after a revocable divorce]." This narration is collected by Al-Tirmidhi in his *Jami'* (no. 1099) and Ibn Majah in his *Sunan* (no. 2028) and graded *Hasan* by Al-Albani in *Sahih Al-Tirmidhi* (no. 1183).

[2] Refer to http://www.alfawzan.af.org.sa/node/13728

[3] Abd Al-Aziz B. Baz, "What Is the Ruling on Jesting in Divorce," www.binbaz.org.sa (accessed June 1, 2024).

The Impermissibility of Lying in Jest

عَنْ معاوية بن حيدة، قَالَ: سَمِعْتُ النَّبِيَّ صَلَّى اللهُ عَلَيْهِ وَسَلَّمَ يَقُولُ: وَيْلٌ لِلَّذِي يُحَدِّثُ بِالحَدِيثِ لِيُضْحِكَ بِهِ القَوْمَ فَيَكْذِبُ، وَيْلٌ لَهُ وَيْلٌ لَهُ.

Mu'awiyah b. Haydah said, "I heard the Messenger of Allah say, 'Woe to those who lie in their speech to make people laugh. Woe to them! Woe to them!'"[1]

Al-Mubarakfuri said, "The expression 'Woe to them!' implies complete destruction or a severe punishment like a deep valley in Hell. It is understood that if a person speaks the truth to bring laughter, it is permissible. 'Umar exemplified this when he was upset with the Mothers of the Believers in the presence of the Prophet ﷺ. Al-Ghazali mentioned that such humor should align with the Prophet's conduct, meaning it should be truthful, considerate of others' feelings, and not excessive. So, if you, O listener, engage in occasional humor, there is no objection."[2]

Imam Al-Manawi said, "He repeated, 'Woe to them! Woe to them!' to highlight the severity of the person's loss. Lying is the root cause of every wrongdoing and represents the height of degradation. Combined with the pursuit of laughter, which numbs the heart, fosters forgetfulness, and encourages frivolity, it becomes even more shameful."[3]

---

[1] Related by Al-Tirmidhi in his *Jami'* (no. 2315) and Abu Dawud in his *Sunan* (no. 4990). It is graded *Hasan* by Al-Albani in *Sahih Al-Targhib wa Al-Tarhib* (no. 2944).
[2] Refer to *Tuhfah Al-Ahwadhi* (6/497).
[3] Refer to *Fayd Al-Qadir* (6/368).

Also, Abu Umamah reported that the Messenger of Allah ﷺ said,

عَنْ أَبِي أُمَامَة، قَالَ: قَالَ رَسُولُ اللهِ صَلَّى اللهُ عَلَيْهِ وَسَلَّمَ: «أَنَا زَعِيمٌ بِبَيْتٍ فِي رَبَضِ الْجَنَّةِ لِمَنْ تَرَكَ الْمِرَاءَ وَإِنْ كَانَ مُحِقًّا، وَبِبَيْتٍ فِي وَسَطِ الْجَنَّةِ لِمَنْ تَرَكَ الْكَذِبَ وَإِنْ كَانَ مَازِحًا وَبِبَيْتٍ فِي أَعْلَى الْجَنَّةِ لِمَنْ حَسَّنَ خُلُقَهُ»

"I guarantee a house in the outskirts of Paradise for whoever leaves argumentation even if he is right, a house in the middle of Paradise for whoever leaves lying even if he is joking, and a house in the highest part of Paradise for whoever has good character."[1]

---

[1] Collected by Abu Dawud in his *Sunan* (no. 4800). *Shaykh* Al-Albani graded it *Hasan* in *Silsilah Al-Ahadith Al-Sahihah* (no. 273).

The Impermissibility of Frightening a Person when Joking

عَنْ عَبْدِ الرَّحْمَنِ بْنِ أَبِي لَيْلَى، قَالَ: حَدَّثَنَا أَصْحَابُ مُحَمَّدٍ صَلَّى اللهُ عَلَيْهِ وَسَلَّمَ، أَنَّهُمْ كَانُوا يَسِيرُونَ مَعَ النَّبِيِّ صَلَّى اللهُ عَلَيْهِ وَسَلَّمَ، فَنَامَ رَجُلٌ مِنْهُمْ، فَانْطَلَقَ بَعْضُهُمْ إِلَى حَبْلٍ مَعَهُ فَأَخَذَهُ، فَفَزِعَ، فَقَالَ رَسُولُ اللهِ صَلَّى اللهُ عَلَيْهِ وَسَلَّمَ: لَا يَحِلُّ لِمُسْلِمٍ أَنْ يُرَوِّعَ مُسْلِمًا

'Abd Al-Rahman b. Abu Layla said, "Some of the Prophet's companions informed us that when they were traveling with him, one of them fell asleep, and someone seized his rope, startling him awake. The Messenger of Allah ﷺ said, 'It is not permissible for a Muslim to frighten another Muslim.'"[1]

Imam Ahmad collects a similar wording:

عَنْ عَبْدِ الرَّحْمَنِ بْنِ أَبِي لَيْلَى قَالَ: حَدَّثَنَا أَصْحَابُ رَسُولِ اللهِ صَلَّى اللهُ عَلَيْهِ وَسلمَ، أَنَّهُمْ كَانُوا يَسِيرُونَ مَعَ رَسُولِ اللهِ صَلَّى اللهُ عَلَيْهِ وَسَلَّمَ فِي مَسِيرٍ، فَنَامَ رَجُلٌ مِنْهُمْ، فَانْطَلَقَ بَعْضُهُمْ إِلَى نَبْلٍ مَعَهُ فَأَخَذَهَا، فَلَمَّا اسْتَيْقَظَ الرَّجُلُ فَزِعَ، فَضَحِكَ الْقَوْمُ، فَقَالَ: مَا يُضْحِكُكُمْ؟ ، فَقَالُوا: لَا، إِلَّا أَنَّا أَخَذْنَا نَبْلَ هَذَا فَفَزِعَ، فَقَالَ رَسُولُ اللهِ صَلَّى اللهُ عَلَيْهِ وَسَلَّمَ: لَا يَحِلُّ لِمُسْلِمٍ أَنْ يُرَوِّعَ مُسْلِمًا

"While they were on a journey with the Prophet, one of them fell asleep. Someone took his rope, and the people laughed when he woke up startled. [The Prophet] said, 'What made you laugh?' Someone replied, 'We took his rope, and he woke up

---

[1] Related by Abu Dawud in his *Sunan* (no. 4333). It is authenticated by Al-Albani in *Sahih Targhib wa Al-Tarhib* (no. 2508).

startled.' So the Messenger of Allah ﷺ said, 'It is not permissible for a Muslim to frighten another Muslim.'"[1]

Finally, *Al-Muhaddith* Muhammad Nasir Al-Din Al-Albani said, "In ['The Chapter of Joking'] and the *hadiths* mentioned by the author,[2] may Allah have mercy on him, it is indicated that jesting is permitted in the *Shariah* as long as it is lawful and truthful. If it is truthful, then it is permissible. However, if it involves harm or injury to a Muslim, it is forbidden. As mentioned in a previous *hadith* of the Prophet: 'None of you should take his brother's stick in jest,' as it instills fear and anxiety in the heart of a Muslim, which is clearly harmful. Yet, truthful joking is harmless."[3]

[1] Related by Ahmad in *Al-Musnad* (no. 24228). It is authenticated by Al-Albani in *Sahih Al-Jami'* (no. 7658).
[2] This refers to *Imam* Al-Bukhari in *Al-Adab Al-Mufrad*.
[3] Muhammad Nasir Al-Din Al-Albani, "Explanation of the Chapter of Joking," accessed June 11,
2024 https://alathar.net/home/esound/index.php?op=codevi&coid=258489.

The Impermissibility of Backbiting when Joking

Allah reproaches backbiting, even in jest.

يَٰٓأَيُّهَا ٱلَّذِينَ ءَامَنُوا۟ ٱجْتَنِبُوا۟ كَثِيرًا مِّنَ ٱلظَّنِّ إِنَّ بَعْضَ ٱلظَّنِّ إِثْمٌ ۖ وَلَا تَجَسَّسُوا۟ وَلَا يَغْتَب بَّعْضُكُم بَعْضًا ۚ أَيُحِبُّ أَحَدُكُمْ أَن يَأْكُلَ لَحْمَ أَخِيهِ مَيْتًا فَكَرِهْتُمُوهُ ۚ وَٱتَّقُوا۟ ٱللَّهَ ۚ إِنَّ ٱللَّهَ تَوَّابٌ رَّحِيمٌ

> "O you who believe! Avoid much suspicion. Indeed, some suspicions are sins. And do not spy or backbite one another. Would one of you like to eat the flesh of his dead brother? You would abhor it [so hate backbiting]. And fear Allah. Indeed, Allah is the One Who accepts repentance, Most Merciful."

> [*Al-Hujurat* 49:12]

Al-Hafiz Ibn Kathir mentions that backbiting is prohibited, as the Messenger of Allah ﷺ clarified. When asked about backbiting, he ﷺ said, "It is to mention something about your brother that he dislikes." "What if it is true?" someone asked. The Prophet responded, "If it is true, you have backbitten him, and if it is false, you have slandered him."[1]

'Aishah illustrates this in her statement, "I said something about Safiyyah,"[2] hinting at [Safiyyah's] short stature. So the

---

[1] Related by Muslim in his *Sahih* (no. 4213).
[2] Related by Abu Dawud in his *Sunan* (no. 4875). It has been authenticated by Al-Albani in *Sahih Abu Dawud* (no. 4875)

51

Messenger of Allah ﷺ said, "You have said a word that would change the ocean if mixed with it."[1]

Also, Hasan b. Al-Makhariq reported that a woman visited 'Aishah, and upon leaving, 'Aishah signaled the Prophet about her short stature. The Prophet then said, "You have backbitten her."[2] Backbiting is prohibited, except in cases of overwhelming benefit, such as in matters of *Al-Jarh wa Al-Ta'dil* (the science of praise and criticism) and when giving advice.[3]

---

[1] Ibid.
[2] Refer to *Tafsir Al-Tabari* (16/136).
[3] Refer to *Tafsir Al-Qur'an Al-Azim* (13/158-160) by Ibn Kathir.

The Impermissibility of Mockery and Derision in Joking

Allah says,

﴿يَـٰٓأَيُّهَا ٱلَّذِينَ ءَامَنُوا لَا يَسْخَرْ قَوْمٌ مِّن قَوْمٍ عَسَىٰٓ أَن يَكُونُوا خَيْرًا مِّنْهُمْ وَلَا نِسَآءٌ مِّن نِّسَآءٍ عَسَىٰٓ أَن يَكُنَّ خَيْرًا مِّنْهُنَّ ۖ وَلَا تَلْمِزُوٓا أَنفُسَكُمْ وَلَا تَنَابَزُوا بِٱلْأَلْقَـٰبِ ۖ بِئْسَ ٱلِٱسْمُ ٱلْفُسُوقُ بَعْدَ ٱلْإِيمَـٰنِ ۚ وَمَن لَّمْ يَتُبْ فَأُوْلَـٰٓئِكَ هُمُ ٱلظَّـٰلِمُونَ﴾

"O you who have believed, let not a people ridicule another people; perhaps they may be better than them; nor let women ridicule other women; perhaps they may be better. Do not insult one another, and do not call each other by offensive nicknames. Wretched is the name of disobedience after one's faith. And whoever does not repent - then it is those who are the wrongdoers." [Al-Hujurat 49:11]

Imam Al-Sa'di stated that mocking fellow Muslims is prohibited, as it demonstrates arrogance and may indicate that the person being mocked is actually superior. Mockery stems from a heart filled with evil traits and is impermissible.[1]

He also states that Allah's command to "not ridicule another people" encompasses verbal defamation and actions of mockery, both of which are forbidden and carry the threat of Hellfire.[2]

---

[1] *Taysir Al-Karim Al-Rahman* (p. 801)
[2] Ibid.

Further, Allah prohibits insulting and using offensive nicknames for fellow believers, as this constitutes derision. However, he clarifies that this prohibition excludes acceptable nicknames.[1]

---

[1] Ibid.

For example, the companion ʿAbd Allah was called *Himar* (donkey). Regarding this, *Al-Hafiz* Badr al-Din al-ʿAyni said, "Perhaps he did not dislike the nickname and had become known by it." Refer to *ʿUmdah al-Qari* (23/270).

Advice Against Joking with the People of Innovation

Some scholars of the *Sunnah* caution against joking with people of innovation, as this typically signifies openness and warmth.

Someone asked *Shaykh* Ahmad b. Yahya al-Najmi, "O *Shaykh*, what is your advice to the *Salafis* in Oman amidst the *Khawarij* and different sects? How should they interact with these groups and factions?"

He answered, "The worshipper must fear Allah and uphold His command to the best of his ability. Allah states,

$$\text{فَٱتَّقُوا۟ ٱللَّهَ مَا ٱسْتَطَعْتُمْ وَٱسْمَعُوا۟ وَأَطِيعُوا۟ وَأَنفِقُوا۟ خَيْرًا لِّأَنفُسِكُمْ ۗ وَمَن يُوقَ شُحَّ نَفْسِهِ فَأُو۟لَـٰٓئِكَ هُمُ ٱلْمُفْلِحُونَ}$$

"Fear Allah to the best of your ability." [*Al-Taghabun*: 64:16]

If compelled to interact with such groups, one should maintain a business-like distance, avoiding cheerfulness, conversation, joking, and similar interactions. I consider this obligatory."[1]

---

[1] *Fath Al-Rahim Al-Wadud* (p. 253)

Section Three: A Glimpse at the Prophet's Humor

Hadith One: "I Only Speak the Truth"

As previously mentioned, there are established principles for joking under Islamic teachings. These principles emphasize the importance of speaking truth and avoiding lies. It is a common misconception that fiction is funnier than fact. However, this belief contradicts the Prophet's guidance, which is the best guidance.

عَنْ أَبِي هُرَيْرَةَ قَالَ: قَالُوا: يَا رَسُولَ اللهِ، إِنَّكَ تُدَاعِبُنَا، قَالَ: إِنِّي لاَ أَقُولُ إِلاَّ حَقًّا.

Abu Hurayrah reported that some companions asked the Prophet ﷺ, "O Messenger of Allah, do you joke with us?"

"Yes," he answered, "but I only tell the truth."[1]

Imam al-Manawi clarified the Prophet's statement, "I only tell the truth," by emphasizing his infallibility in words and deeds. While the Prophet ﷺ occasionally joked, he did so to ease the burden of following his way. It would have contradicted human nature if he had always been serious. So, the Prophet ﷺ used humor to create a joyful atmosphere and encourage others to do likewise.[2]

Finally, a questioner asked *Shaykh* Al-Albani, "What is the ruling on lying in jest?"

---

[1] Related by Al-Tirmidhi in his *Jami'* (no. 1990). It is authenticated by Al-Albani in *Silsilah Al-Ahadith Al-Sahihah* (no. 1726).
[2] Refer to *Fayd Al-Qadir* (3/18).

"What's that?" *Shaykh* Al-Albani said.

"Lying in jest, like using euphemisms, what is its ruling?"

"I don't understand," *Shaykh* Al-Albani said.

"Lying in jest?" another questioner said.

"Yes."

"It's a forgivable lie! (Everyone laughs.) Do you think jesting permits lying?" *Shaykh* Al-Albani said.

"Euphemisms and indirect expressions?" the questioner said.

"Euphemisms and indirect expressions - may Allah bless you - differ from jesting. Lying in jest is perhaps worse than lying...Do you know why? Because the Prophet used to joke, but he only told the truth. So, if someone jokes *and* lies, they are sinning and going against the practice of the Prophet, who joked but always told the truth.

Using euphemisms and indirect expressions is different. If there is a necessity to use them, it is better than outright lying. However, when should one do that? Only when there is a need. It is also impermissible if someone does so without reason or necessity."[1]

---

[1] Muhammad Nasir Al-Din Al-Albani, "حكم الكذب في المزاح واستعمال الكناية والمعاريض," accessed June 10, 2024, https://www.al-albany.com/audios/content/141672/.

Hadith Two: "O Abu ʿUmayr!"

عَنْ أَبِي التَّيَّاحِ الضُّبَعِيّ قَالَ: سَمِعْتُ أَنَسَ بْنَ مَالِكٍ يَقُولُ: كَانَ رَسُولُ اللهِ صَلَّى اللهُ
عَلَيْهِ وَسَلَّمَ يُخَالِطُنَا، حَتَّى كَانَ يَقُولُ لِأَخٍ لِي صَغِيرٍ: يَا أَبَا عُمَيْرٍ مَا فَعَلَ النُّغَيْرُ.

Anas b. Malik reported, "The Prophet would spend time with us and [joke with us]. On one occasion, he asked my younger brother,[1] 'O, father of ʿUmayr, what happened to *Al-Nughayr* (the small bird)?'"[2]

Imam Al-Tirmidhi stated, "This narration shows the Prophet's humorous side, calling this young one 'father of ʿUmayr.' It also highlights that there is no harm in giving children birds as pets. In this specific incident, the boy had a pet bird that unfortunately died, causing him great sadness. To console him, the Prophet ﷺ jokingly asked about the bird, saying, 'O father of ʿUmayr, what happened to *Al-Nughayr*?'"[3]

---

[1] *Shaykh* Al-Albani stated, "He is Ibn Abu Talhah Zayd b. Sahl Al-Ansari, Anas's maternal brother. Their mother's name is Umm Sulaym bint Milhan. Abu ʿUmayr died as a youth during the life of the Prophet." Refer to *Mukhtasar Al-Shamaʾil Al-Muhammadiyyah* (p. 125).

[2] Related by Al-Tirmidhi in his *Jamiʿ* (no. 1991). He says, "This *hadith* is *Hasan Sahih*." *Shaykh* Al-Albani states, "Al-Tirmidhi's statement is correct, as I have clarified in *Al-Sahihah*" (no. 1762).

[3] *Mukhtasar Al-Shamaʾil Al-Muhammadiyyah* (pp. 125-126).

Hadith Three: "O Two-Eared One!"

عَنْ أَنَسٍ، قَالَ: رُبَّمَا قَالَ لِيَ النَّبِيُّ صَلَّى اللّٰهُ عَلَيْهِ وَسَلَّمَ: يَا ذَا الْأُذُنَيْنِ. قَالَ أَبُو أُسَامَةَ: يَعْنِي يُمَازِحُهُ.

Anas b. Malik reported, "The Prophet said to me, 'O, you with two ears.'"[1] Abu Usamah[2] said, "He said this jokingly."

'Abd Al-Rahman Al-Mubarakfuri said, "Some say this exemplifies the Prophet's humorous and gentle demeanor, as stated by the author of *Al-Nihayah*. This is apparent to me and aligns with the understanding of Al-Tirmidhi and his *Shaykh* (i.e. Abu Usamah)."[3] [4]

---

[1] Related by Al-Tirmidhi in his *Jami'* (no. 1993) and Abu Dawud in his *Sunan* (no. 5002). Al-Albani authenticated it in *Al-Shama'il* (p. 125).
[2] One of the narrators in the chain of transmission.
[3] Refer to *'Awn Al-Ma'bud* (13/235).
[4] Refer to *Tuhfah Al-Ahwadhi* (6/108).

Hadith Four: "Your Pillow Is Wide Indeed"

عَنْ عَدِيِّ بْنِ حَاتِمٍ رَضِيَ اللهُ عَنْهُ، قَالَ: لما نَزَلَتْ: ﴿حَتَّى يَتَبَيَّنَ لَكُمُ الْخَيْطُ الْأَبْيَضُ مِنَ الْخَيْطِ الْأَسْوَدِ مِنَ الْفَجْرِ﴾ [البقرة: 187] قَالَ لَهُ عَدِيُّ بْنُ حَاتِمٍ: يَا رَسُولَ اللهِ، إِنِّي أَجْعَلُ تَحْتَ وِسَادَتِي عِقَالَيْنِ: عِقَالًا أَبْيَضَ وَعِقَالًا أَسْوَدَ، أَعْرِفُ اللَّيْلَ مِنَ النَّهَارِ، فَقَالَ رَسُولُ اللهِ صَلَّى اللهُ عَلَيْهِ وَسَلَّمَ: «إِنَّ وِسَادَتَكَ لَعَرِيضٌ، إِنَّمَا هُوَ سَوَادُ اللَّيْلِ، وَبَيَاضُ النَّهَارِ»

'Adiyy b. Hatim said, "When the verse, 'Until the white thread of dawn is distinct to you from the black thread,' was revealed, I said, 'O Messenger of Allah, I keep a white and a black thread under my pillow to discern day and night.'

'Your pillow is wide indeed. The true threads are night's darkness and day's light.'"[1]

Al-Qadi 'Iyad said, "If a pillow covers the threads of day and night, it suggests its vastness exceeds their boundaries. This is like another narration in Al-Bukhari that says, 'You must have a large nape,' as having such a big pillow implies having an equally large nape."[2]

---

[1] Collected by Al-Bukhari in his *Sahih* (no. 1782) and Muslim in his *Sahih* (no. 1816).
[2] *Sharh Muslim* (2/766)

Hadith Five: "No Old Woman Will Enter Paradise"

عن الحسن قال: أَتَتْ عَجُوزٌ إِلَى النَّبِيِّ صَلَّى اللهُ عَلَيْهِ وَسَلَّمَ فَقَالَتْ: يَا رَسُولَ اللهِ
ادْعُ اللهَ أَنْ يُدْخِلَنِي الْجَنَّةَ. فَقَالَ: (يَا أُمَّ فُلَانٍ إِنَّ الْجَنَّةَ لَا تَدْخُلُهَا عَجُوزٌ). قَالَ:
فَوَلَّتْ تَبْكِي. فَقَالَ: (أَخْبِرُوهَا أَنَّهَا لَا تَدْخُلُهَا وَهِيَ عَجُوزٌ إِنَّ اللهَ تَعَالَى يَقُولُ: إِنَّا
أَنْشَأْنَاهُنَّ إِنْشَاءً. فَجَعَلْنَاهُنَّ أَبْكَارًا. عربا أترابا)

Hasan Al-Basri said, "An old woman came to the Prophet and made a request: 'O Messenger of Allah, supplicate that Allah allows me to enter Paradise.' Allah's Messenger ﷺ replied, 'O' Mother of so-and-so, an old woman cannot enter Paradise.' The woman walked away weeping. The Prophet said, 'Inform her she will not enter as an old woman.

Allah says,

$$﴿ إِنَّا أَنْشَأْنَاهُنَّ إِنْشَاءً ٣٥ فَجَعَلْنَاهُنَّ أَبْكَارًا ﴾$$

"Lo! We have created them a new creation and made them virgins, lovers, equal in age.'"

[*Al-Waqi'ah* 56:35-36][1]

---

[1] Refer to Al-Tirmidhi's *Al-Shama'il* (no. 205). This narration has been graded *hasan* (sound) by *Imam* Al-Albani. In his *mukhtasar* (summary) of *Al-Shama'il*, he comments, "Its chain is weak. Along with the *irsal* chain of Al-Hasan [Al-Basri], the narrator Al-Mubarik b. Fadalah is *mudallis* and has used *'an'anah* here. It is also collected in *Ghayah Al-Maram fi Takhrij Ahadith Al-Halal wa Al-Haram* (no. 375), and I have graded it *hasan* there based on a supporting narration."

Hadith Six: "Zahir Is Our Desert"

عَنْ أَنَسٍ، أَنَّ رَجُلًا مِنْ أَهْلِ الْبَادِيَةِ كَانَ اسْمُهُ زَاهِرًا، وَكَانَ يُهْدِي إِلَى رَسُولِ اللَّهِ صَلَّى اللَّهُ عَلَيْهِ وَسَلَّمَ مِنَ الْبَادِيَةِ، فَيُجَهِّزُهُ رَسُولُ اللَّهِ صَلَّى اللَّهُ عَلَيْهِ وَسَلَّمَ إِذَا أَرَادَ أَنْ يَخْرُجَ، فَقَالَ النَّبِيُّ صَلَّى اللَّهُ عَلَيْهِ وَسَلَّمَ: «إِنَّ زَاهِرًا بَادِيَتُنَا، وَنَحْنُ حَاضِرُوهُ» . وَكَانَ النَّبِيُّ صَلَّى اللَّهُ عَلَيْهِ وَسَلَّمَ يُحِبُّهُ، وَكَانَ رَجُلًا دَمِيمًا، فَأَتَاهُ النَّبِيُّ صَلَّى اللَّهُ عَلَيْهِ وَسَلَّمَ يَوْمًا وَهُوَ يَبِيعُ مَتَاعَهُ، فَاحْتَضَنَهُ مِنْ خَلْفِهِ وَلَا يُبْصِرُهُ الرَّجُلُ، فَقَالَ: أَرْسِلْنِي مَنْ هَذَا، فَالْتَفَتَ فَعَرَفَ النَّبِيَّ صَلَّى اللَّهُ عَلَيْهِ وَسَلَّمَ، فَجَعَلَ لَا يَأْلُو مَا أَلْصَقَ ظَهْرَهُ بِصَدْرِ النَّبِيِّ صَلَّى اللَّهُ عَلَيْهِ وَسَلَّمَ، حِينَ عَرَفَهُ، وَجَعَلَ النَّبِيُّ صَلَّى اللَّهُ عَلَيْهِ وَسَلَّمَ يَقُولُ: «مَنْ يَشْتَرِي الْعَبْدَ؟» فَقَالَ: يَا رَسُولَ اللَّهِ، إِذًا وَاللَّهِ تَجِدُنِي كَاسِدًا، فَقَالَ النَّبِيُّ صَلَّى اللَّهُ عَلَيْهِ وَسَلَّمَ: لَكِنْ عِنْدَ اللَّهِ لَسْتَ بِكَاسِدٍ أَوْ قَالَ: «لَكِنْ عِنْدَ اللَّهِ أَنْتَ غَالٍ»

Anas b. Malik said that a Bedouin named Zahir used to bring the Prophet gifts from the desert. Whenever he intended to leave, Allah's Messenger would give him things. The Prophet said, "Zahir is our desert, and we are his town." Allah's Messenger loved him, though he was a homely man. Once, the Prophet came to him while he was selling his wares and grabbed him from behind so that Zahir could not see him. Zahir said, "Who is this? Let go of me." Then he turned around and recognized the Prophet. Once he realized it was Allah's Messenger, he stopped struggling and leaned his back against the Prophet's chest. Allah's Apostle said, "Who will buy this slave?"

"O Messenger of Allah, in that case, you will find me a worthless commodity," Zahir said.

"To Allah, you are valuable," the Prophet said.[1]

The word "slave" can be understood literally, as he is a slave of Allah. However, the narration does not imply an actual sale, especially since it was said humorously and because selling a free person is impermissible. Allah knows best.[2]

---

[1] Related by *Imam* Ahmad in his *Musnad* (no. 12749). It is authenticated by Al-Albani in *Mukhtasar Al-Shama'il* (p. 127).
[2] Refer to *Jam' Al-Wasail fi Sharh Al-Shamail* (2/30).

Hadith Seven: "Isn't Every Camel the Calf of a She-Camel?"

عَنْ أَنَسِ بْنِ مَالِكٍ، أَنَّ رَجُلاً اسْتَحْمَلَ رَسُولَ اللهِ صَلَّى اللهُ عَلَيْهِ وَسَلَّمَ فَقَالَ: إِنِّي
حَامِلُكَ عَلَى وَلَدِ النَّاقَةِ فَقَالَ: يَا رَسُولَ اللهِ، مَا أَصْنَعُ بِوَلَدِ النَّاقَةِ؟ فَقَالَ رَسُولُ اللهِ
صَلَّى اللهُ عَلَيْهِ وَسَلَّمَ: وَهَلْ تَلِدُ الإِبِلَ إِلاَّ النُّوقُ.

Anas b. Malik reported that a man asked the Prophet to provide him with a camel to ride. So, the Prophet said, "I will give you a she-camel's calf."

"O Messenger of Allah, what will I do with a calf?" he replied.

"Isn't every camel the calf of a she-camel?" the Prophet responded.[1]

Al-Azim Abadi said, "Even full-grown camels are the offspring of she-camels. Therefore, it is correct to say 'the she-camel's calf' no matter the size.[2] Al-Bayjuri stated this in *Sharh Al-Shama'il*." Al-Azim Abadi added that this narration and subsequent traditions in this chapter illustrate the permissibility of joking. The Messenger of Allah ﷺ joked with his companions but always told the truth.[3]

Al-Mubarakfuri said, "As for the Prophet's statement, 'We will give you a she-camel's calf [to ride],' he said this to him

---

[1] Related by Al-Tirmidhi in his *Jami'* (no. 724), Abu Dawud in his *Sunan* (no. 4328), and Ahmad in his *Musnad* (no. 13926). It has been authenticated by Al-Albani in *Mukhtasar Al-Shama'il* (p. 126).

[2] This is like an old woman calling her adult son her "oldest child." Despite his age, she still refers to him this way. The Prophet ﷺ used this type of wordplay in the narration.

[3] Refer to *'Awn Al-Ma'bud* (13/282).

jokingly…[The companion] mistakenly thought that the word 'calf' is only used for the young [camel] and therefore not suitable for riding. His statement, 'Isn't every camel the calf of a she-camel?' means its type, regardless of the size. So, if you had reflected, you would not have responded this way.

Along with joking, the Prophet ﷺ showed us that when one hears a statement, he should reflect upon it and not respond until he has [completely] understood it."[1]

---

[1] Refer to *Tuhfah Al-Ahwadhi* (6/109).

Hadith Eight: "O Unays! Did You Go Where I Sent You?"

قَالَ أَنَسٌ: كَانَ رَسُولُ اللهِ صَلَّى اللهُ عَلَيْهِ وَسَلَّمَ مِنْ أَحْسَنِ النَّاسِ خُلُقًا، فَأَرْسَلَنِي يَوْمًا لِحَاجَةٍ، فَقُلْتُ: وَاللهِ لَا أَذْهَبُ، وَفِي نَفْسِي أَنْ أَذْهَبَ لِمَا أَمَرَنِي بِهِ نَبِيُّ اللهِ صَلَّى اللهُ عَلَيْهِ وَسَلَّمَ، فَخَرَجْتُ حَتَّى أَمُرَّ عَلَى صِبْيَانٍ وَهُمْ يَلْعَبُونَ فِي السُّوقِ، فَإِذَا رَسُولُ اللهِ صَلَّى اللهُ عَلَيْهِ وَسَلَّمَ قَدْ قَبَضَ بِقَفَايَ مِنْ وَرَائِي، قَالَ: فَنَظَرْتُ إِلَيْهِ وَهُوَ يَضْحَكُ، فَقَالَ: يَا أُنَيْسُ أَذَهَبْتَ حَيْثُ أَمَرْتُكَ؟ قَالَ قُلْتُ: نَعَمْ، أَنَا أَذْهَبُ، يَا رَسُولَ اللهِ. و قال: واللهِ لقد خدَمْتُه سبعَ سنين – أو تسعَ سنين – ما علمتُ قال لشيءٍ صنعْتُ: لِمَ فَعَلْتَ كذا وكذا ، ولا لشيءٍ تَرَكْتَ: هلَّا فعلتَ كذا وكذا.

Anas said, "The Messenger of Allah ﷺ had the most excellent character. One day, he sent me on an errand, but I said, 'By Allah, I will not go.' Yet, I was determined to go because the Prophet had commanded me to do so. On my way, I passed a group of children playing in the market. By and by, Allah's Messenger gripped my neck from behind. When I looked at him, he was laughing and said, 'O Unays![1] Did you go where I sent you?' I said, 'I am on my way, O Messenger of Allah.'"

Anas then stated, "I served the Prophet for ten years. During that time, he never uttered a word of disapproval, neither saying 'why did you do that?' nor 'why didn't you do that?'"[2]

---

[1] This means "little Anas," the diminutive form of his name. It is a way of showing closeness and affection to a loved one.

[2] Related by Muslim in his *Sahih* (no. 4251) and Abu Dawud in his *Sunan* (no. 4125).

Al-Ḥāfiẓ al-Nawawi said, "This *hadith* demonstrates the Prophet's completeness of character, excellent companionship, and remarkable forbearance."[1]

Imam al-Qurtubi said, "Anas's statement, 'By Allah, I will not go. Yet I was determined to go because the Prophet had commanded me to do so,' came from him during his youth, before the age of discernment, as it would not come from someone who had reached maturity...Also, the Messenger of Allah ﷺ did not reprimand him for this. Instead, he joked with him, taking him by the neck and laughing out of friendliness and kindness. Then he said, 'O Unays! Did you go where I sent you?' He replied, 'I am going.' This is due to [the Prophet's] noble character and great patience."[2]

---

[1] Refer to *Sharḥ Ṣaḥīḥ Muslim* (8/79).
[2] Refer to *Al-Mufhim* (6/104).

Hadith Nine: The Redness of His Tongue

، عَنْ أَبِي هُرَيْرَةَ: أَنَّ النَّبِيَّ صَلَّى اللهُ عَلَيْهِ وَسَلَّمَ كَانَ يدلع لِسَانه للحسين بْن عَلِيّ
فَإِذا رَأَى الصَّبِي حمرَة لِسَانه، يهش إِلَيْهِ.

Abu Hurayrah said, "The Messenger of Allah ﷺ used to playfully stick out his tongue at Al-Hasan b. ʿAli, and when the boy saw its redness, he would come running to him."[1]

This narration illustrates the Prophet's playful, loving nature with children, especially his grandsons. It also teaches us the importance of spending time with and amusing our young ones. There is no shame in this. Rather, it is from the *Sunnah*.

---

[1] Related by Al-Baghawi in *Sharh Al-Sunnah* (13/180) and Abu Al-Shaykh in *Akhlaq Al-Nabi* (no. 178). This narration's chain has been graded *Hasan* by Al-Albani in *Silsilah Al-Ahadith Al-Sahihah* (no. 70).

Hadith Ten: "So You Could Amuse Her"

عَنْ جَابِرِ بْنِ عَبْدِ اللهِ، أَنَّ عَبْدَ اللهِ هَلَكَ، وَتَرَكَ تِسْعَ بَنَاتٍ – أَوْ قَالَ سَبْعَ –
فَتَزَوَّجْتُ امْرَأَةً ثَيِّبًا، فَقَالَ لِي رَسُولُ اللهِ صَلَّى اللهُ عَلَيْهِ وَسَلَّمَ: «يَا جَابِرُ،
تَزَوَّجْتَ؟» قَالَ: قُلْتُ: نَعَمْ، قَالَ: «فَبِكْرٌ، أَمْ ثَيِّبٌ؟» قَالَ: قُلْتُ: بَلْ ثَيِّبٌ يَا
رَسُولَ اللهِ، قَالَ: «فَهَلَّا جَارِيَةً تُلَاعِبُهَا وَتُلَاعِبُكَ»، أَوْ قَالَ: «تُضَاحِكُهَا
وَتُضَاحِكُكَ»، قَالَ: قُلْتُ لَهُ: إِنَّ عَبْدَ اللهِ هَلَكَ، وَتَرَكَ تِسْعَ بَنَاتٍ – أَوْ سَبْعَ –،
وَإِنِّي كَرِهْتُ أَنْ آتِيَهُنَّ أَوْ أَجِيئَهُنَّ بِمِثْلِهِنَّ، فَأَحْبَبْتُ أَنْ أَجِيءَ بِامْرَأَةٍ تَقُومُ عَلَيْهِنَّ،
وَتُصْلِحُهُنَّ، قَالَ: «فَبَارَكَ اللهُ لَكَ»

Jabir b. 'Abd Allah said, "My father died and left me with seven or nine daughters, so I married a *thayyib* (a divorcée).

The Messenger of Allah ﷺ said, 'Have you married, O Jabir?'

'Yes,' I replied.

'A virgin or a divorcée?' he said.

'A divorcée.'

'Why didn't you marry a virgin with whom you could have played and had fun together?' he said.

''Abd Allah (i.e. my father) has died, and I disliked marrying someone similar to them. So instead, I married a woman to help rear them.'

'May Allah bless you,' he said."[1]

In another wording collected by Muslim, he said,

عَنْ جَابِرِ بْنِ عَبْدِ اللهِ، قَالَ: كُنَّا فِي مَسِيرٍ مَعَ رَسُولِ اللهِ صَلَّى اللهُ عَلَيْهِ وَسَلَّمَ، وَأَنَا
عَلَى نَاضِحٍ، إِنَّمَا هُوَ فِي أُخْرَيَاتِ النَّاسِ، قَالَ: فَضَرَبَهُ رَسُولُ اللهِ صَلَّى اللهُ عَلَيْهِ
وَسَلَّمَ – أَوْ قَالَ: نَخَسَهُ، أُرَاهُ قَالَ: بِشَيْءٍ كَانَ مَعَهُ – قَالَ: فَجَعَلَ بَعْدَ ذَلِكَ يَتَقَدَّمُ
النَّاسَ يُنَازِعُنِي، حَتَّى إِنِّي لَأَكُفُّهُ، قَالَ: فَقَالَ رَسُولُ اللهِ صَلَّى اللهُ عَلَيْهِ وَسَلَّمَ:
«أَتَبِيعُنِيهِ بِكَذَا وَكَذَا وَاللَّهُ يَغْفِرُ لَكَ؟» قَالَ: قُلْتُ: هُوَ لَكَ يَا نَبِيَّ اللهِ، قَالَ:
«أَتَبِيعُنِيهِ بِكَذَا وَكَذَا، وَاللهُ يَغْفِرُ لَكَ؟» قَالَ: قُلْتُ: هُوَ لَكَ، يَا نَبِيَّ اللهِ، قَالَ: وَقَالَ
لِي: «أَتَزَوَّجْتَ بَعْدَ أَبِيكَ؟» قُلْتُ: نَعَمْ، قَالَ: «ثَيِّبًا، أَمْ بِكْرًا؟» قَالَ: قُلْتُ: ثَيِّبًا،
قَالَ: «فَهَلَّا تَزَوَّجْتَ بِكْرًا تُضَاحِكُكَ وَتُضَاحِكُهَا، وَتُلَاعِبُكَ وَتُلَاعِبُهَا».

"We were on a journey with Allah's Messenger, and I was riding a camel meant for carrying water. It lagged behind everyone else. Allah's Messenger hit it or prodded it with something he had with him. Afterward, it raced ahead of the people to where I had to hold it back.

The Messenger of Allah ﷺ said, 'Will you sell it at such-and-such [a price]? May Allah grant you pardon.'

'O Allah's Prophet, it is yours,' I said.

'Will you sell it at such-and-such [price]? May Allah grant you pardon,' he repeated.
'O Allah's Prophet, it is yours.'

---

[1] Related by Al-Bukhari in his *Sahih* (no. 5069 and 6029) and Muslim in his *Sahih* (no. 2656).

71

'Have you married after your father's death?' he said.

'Yes,' I replied.

'To a divorcée or a virgin?' he said.

'A divorcée.'

'Why didn't you marry a virgin who might amuse you, and whom you might amuse; who might play with you, and with whom you might play?"'[1]

---

[1] Related by Muslim in his *Sahih* (no. 2659).

Hadith Eleven: "I Am to You as Abu Zar' Was to Umm Zar'"

عَنْ عَائِشَةَ، قَالَتْ: جَلَسَ إِحْدَى عَشْرَةَ امْرَأَةً، فَتَعَاهَدْنَ وَتَعَاقَدْنَ أَنْ لاَ يَكْتُمْنَ مِنْ أَخْبَارِ أَزْوَاجِهِنَّ شَيْئًا، قَالَتِ الأُولَى: زَوْجِي لَحْمُ جَمَلٍ غَثٍّ، عَلَى رَأْسِ جَبَلٍ: لاَ سَهْلٍ فَيُرْتَقَى وَلاَ سَمِينٍ فَيُنْتَقَلُ، قَالَتِ الثَّانِيَةُ: زَوْجِي لاَ أَبُثُّ خَبَرَهُ، إِنِّي أَخَافُ أَنْ لاَ أَذَرَهُ، إِنْ أَذْكُرْهُ أَذْكُرْ عُجَرَهُ وَبُجَرَهُ، قَالَتِ الثَّالِثَةُ: زَوْجِيَ العَشَنَّقُ، إِنْ أَنْطِقْ أُطَلَّقْ وَإِنْ أَسْكُتْ أُعَلَّقْ، قَالَتِ الرَّابِعَةُ: زَوْجِي كَلَيْلِ تِهَامَةَ، لاَ حَرٌّ وَلاَ قُرٌّ، وَلاَ مَخَافَةَ وَلاَ سَآمَةَ، قَالَتِ الخَامِسَةُ: زَوْجِي إِنْ دَخَلَ فَهِدَ، وَإِنْ خَرَجَ أَسِدَ، وَلاَ يَسْأَلُ عَمَّا عَهِدَ، قَالَتِ السَّادِسَةُ: زَوْجِي إِنْ أَكَلَ لَفَّ، وَإِنْ شَرِبَ اشْتَفَّ، وَإِنِ اضْطَجَعَ الْتَفَّ، وَلاَ يُولِجُ الكَفَّ لِيَعْلَمَ البَثَّ. قَالَتِ السَّابِعَةُ: زَوْجِي غَيَايَاءُ – أَوْ عَيَايَاءُ – طَبَاقَاءُ، كُلُّ دَاءٍ لَهُ دَاءٌ، شَجَّكِ أَوْ فَلَّكِ أَوْ جَمَعَ كُلًّا لَكِ، قَالَتِ الثَّامِنَةُ: زَوْجِي المَسُّ مَسُّ أَرْنَبٍ، وَالرِّيحُ رِيحُ زَرْنَبٍ، قَالَتِ التَّاسِعَةُ: زَوْجِي رَفِيعُ العِمَادِ، طَوِيلُ النِّجَادِ، عَظِيمُ الرَّمَادِ، قَرِيبُ البَيْتِ مِنَ النَّادِ، قَالَتِ العَاشِرَةُ: زَوْجِي مَالِكٌ وَمَا مَالِكٌ، مَالِكٌ خَيْرٌ مِنْ ذَلِكِ، لَهُ إِبِلٌ كَثِيرَاتُ المَبَارِكِ، قَلِيلَاتُ المَسَارِحِ، وَإِذَا سَمِعْنَ صَوْتَ المِزْهَرِ، أَيْقَنَّ أَنَّهُنَّ هَوَالِكُ، قَالَتِ الحَادِيَةَ عَشْرَةَ: زَوْجِي أَبُو زَرْعٍ، وَمَا أَبُو زَرْعٍ، أَنَاسَ مِنْ حُلِيٍّ أُذُنَيَّ، وَمَلأَ مِنْ شَحْمٍ عَضُدَيَّ، وَبَجَّحَنِي فَبَجِحَتْ إِلَيَّ نَفْسِي، وَجَدَنِي فِي أَهْلِ غُنَيْمَةٍ بِشِقٍّ، فَجَعَلَنِي فِي أَهْلِ صَهِيلٍ وَأَطِيطٍ، وَدَائِسٍ وَمُنَقٍّ، فَعِنْدَهُ أَقُولُ فَلاَ أُقَبَّحُ، وَأَرْقُدُ فَأَتَصَبَّحُ، وَأَشْرَبُ فَأَتَقَنَّحُ، أُمُّ أَبِي زَرْعٍ، فَمَا أُمُّ أَبِي زَرْعٍ، عُكُومُهَا رَدَاحٌ، وَبَيْتُهَا فَسَاحٌ، ابْنُ أَبِي زَرْعٍ، فَمَا ابْنُ أَبِي زَرْعٍ، مَضْجَعُهُ كَمَسَلِّ شَطْبَةٍ، وَيُشْبِعُهُ ذِرَاعُ الجَفْرَةِ، بِنْتُ أَبِي زَرْعٍ، فَمَا بِنْتُ أَبِي زَرْعٍ، طَوْعُ أَبِيهَا، وَطَوْعُ أُمِّهَا، وَمِلْءُ كِسَائِهَا، وَغَيْظُ جَارَتِهَا، جَارِيَةُ أَبِي زَرْعٍ، فَمَا جَارِيَةُ أَبِي زَرْعٍ، لاَ تَبُثُّ حَدِيثَنَا تَبْثِيثًا، وَلاَ تُنَقِّثُ مِيرَتَنَا تَنْقِيثًا، وَلاَ تَمْلأُ بَيْتَنَا تَعْشِيشًا، قَالَتْ: خَرَجَ أَبُو زَرْعٍ وَالأَوْطَابُ تُمْخَضُ، فَلَقِيَ امْرَأَةً مَعَهَا وَلَدَانِ لَهَا كَالفَهْدَيْنِ، يَلْعَبَانِ مِنْ تَحْتِ خَصْرِهَا بِرُمَّانَتَيْنِ،

73

فَطَلَّقَنِي وَنَكَحَهَا، فَنَكَحْتُ بَعْدَهُ رَجُلًا سَرِيًّا، رَكِبَ شَرِيًّا، وَأَخَذَ خَطِّيًّا، وَأَرَاحَ عَلَيَّ نَعَمًا ثَرِيًّا، وَأَعْطَانِي مِنْ كُلِّ رَائِحَةٍ زَوْجًا، وَقَالَ: كُلِي أُمَّ زَرْعٍ وَمِيرِي أَهْلَكِ، قَالَتْ: فَلَوْ جَمَعْتُ كُلَّ شَيْءٍ أَعْطَانِيهِ، مَا بَلَغَ أَصْغَرَ آنِيَةِ أَبِي زَرْعٍ، قَالَتْ عَائِشَةُ: قَالَ رَسُولُ اللَّهِ صَلَّى اللهُ عَلَيْهِ وَسَلَّمَ: «كُنْتُ لَكِ كَأَبِي زَرْعٍ لِأُمِّ زَرْعٍ».

'Aishah narrated, "Eleven women sat together and promised they would conceal nothing regarding news of their husbands. The first one said, 'My husband is like the meat of a lean, weak camel that is kept on the top of a mountain, which is neither easy to climb nor is the meat fat so that one might put up with the trouble of fetching it.'

The second one said, 'I shall not relate my husband's news, for I fear I may not finish his story. If I describe him, I will mention all his defects and poor traits.'

The third one said, 'My husband is a tall man. If I describe him [and he hears of it], he will divorce me. If I keep quiet, he will neither divorce me nor treat me as a wife.'

The fourth one said, 'My husband is a moderate person, like the night of Tihamah, which is neither hot nor cold. I am neither afraid of him nor discontented with him.'

The fifth one said, 'My husband, when entering [the house], is a leopard, and when leaving, is a lion. He does not ask about whatever is in the house.'

The sixth one said, 'If my husband eats, he overeats (leaving the dishes empty), and if he drinks, he leaves nothing. If he sleeps, he sleeps alone (away from me), covered in garments, and does not stretch his hands here and there to know how I fare.'

The seventh one said, 'My husband is a wrong-doer or weak and foolish. He possesses every defect. He may injure your head or your body or may do both.'

The eighth one said, 'My husband is soft to touch like a rabbit and smells like *zarnab* (a kind of good-smelling grass).'

The ninth one said, 'My husband is a tall, generous man wearing a long strap for carrying his sword. His ashes are abundant, and his house is near the people who would easily consult him.'

The tenth one said, 'My husband is Malik, and what is Malik? Malik is greater than whatever I say about him. (He is beyond and above all praises that can come to my mind.) Most of his camels are kept at home [ready to be slaughtered for the guests], and only a few are taken to the pastures. When the camels hear the lute (or the tambourine), they realize they will be slaughtered for the guests.'

The eleventh one said, 'My husband is Abu Zar', and what is Abu Zar' (i.e., what should I say about him)? He has given me many ornaments. My ears are heavily loaded with them, and my arms have become fat (i.e., I have become fat). He has pleased me, and I have become so happy that I feel proud of myself. He found me with my family, who were mere sheep owners living in poverty, and brought me to a respected family with horses and camels and threshed and purified grain.

Whatever I say, he does not rebuke or insult me. When I sleep, I sleep till late in the morning, and when I drink water [or milk], I drink my fill. The mother of Abu Zar' and what may one say in praise of the mother of Abu Zar'? Her saddle bags are always full of provisions, and her house is spacious.

As for the son of Abu Zar', what may one say about the son of Abu Zar'? His bed is as narrow as an unsheathed sword, and a kid's arm [of four months] satisfies his hunger. As for the daughter of Abu Zar', she is obedient to her father and mother. She has a fat, well-built body, which arouses the jealousy of her husband's other wife.

As for the maidservant of Abu Zar', what may one say about the maidservant of Abu Zar'? She does not uncover our secrets but keeps them, and does not waste our provisions and does not leave garbage scattered everywhere in our house.'

The eleventh lady added, 'One day it so happened that Abu Zar' went out when the animals were being milked, and he saw a woman who had two sons, like two leopards, playing with her breasts. [On seeing her], he divorced me and married her. After that, I married a nobleman who used to ride a fast, tireless horse and keep a spear in his hand. He gave me many things, including a pair of every kind of livestock, and said, 'Eat [of this], O Umm Zar', and give provision to your relatives.' She added, 'Yet, all those things which my second husband gave me could not fill the smallest vessel of Abu Zar's.'"

'Aishah then said, "Allah's Messenger said to me, 'I am to you as Abu Zar' was to Umm Zar'.'"[1]

Regarding the Prophet's statement, "I am to you as Abu Zar' was to Umm Zar'," *Al-Hafiz* Al-Nawawi said, "The scholars say that this delighted her and exemplified his beautiful companionship with her [...] Umm Zar's *hadith* contains several benefits, such as the importance of seeking good companionship within one's family, the permissibility of sharing stories from past nations, and the understanding that comparing two things[2] does not imply they are alike in every aspect."[3]

Al-Hafiz Ibn Hajr stated, "This narration provides several additional benefits, such as the importance of a husband maintaining good companionship with his family through cheerfulness and permissible speech, as long as it does not lead to anything prohibited. It also illustrates the value of occasional humor, light-heartedness, and a husband joking with his family while expressing his love for them."[4]

---

[1] Related by Al-Bukhari in his *Sahih* (no. 4911).
[2] This alludes to the Prophet ﷺ comparing himself to Abu Zar', yet they differ in several ways. For instance, Abu Zar' divorced Umm Zar', whereas the Prophet ﷺ remained with our mother 'Aishah.
[3] *Sharh Sahih* Muslim (8/238).
[4] *Fath Al-Bari* (9/276).

Hadith Twelve: "This Is for the Last Time You Defeated Me"

عَنْ عَائِشَةَ، رَضِيَ اللهُ عَنْهَا، أَنَّهَا كَانَتْ مَعَ النَّبِيِّ صَلَّى اللهُ عَلَيْهِ وَسَلَّمَ فِي سَفَرٍ قَالَتْ: فَسَابَقْتُهُ فَسَبَقْتُهُ عَلَى رِجْلَيَّ، فَلَمَّا حَمَلْتُ اللَّحْمَ سَابَقْتُهُ فَسَبَقَنِي فَقَالَ: «هَذِهِ بِتِلْكَ السَّبْقَةِ»

'Aishah reported that she was on a journey with the Messenger of Allah. She said, "I raced him on foot and defeated him. However, when I grew heavier, I again raced him, and he beat me. He said, 'This is [payback] for the time you defeated me.'"[1]

Another wording states,

عَنْ عَائِشَةَ، قَالَت: خَرَجْتُ مَعَ النَّبِيِّ صَلَّى الله عَلَيْهِ وَسَلَّمَ فِي بَعْضِ أَسْفَارِهِ وَأَنَا جَارِيَةٌ لَمْ أَحْمِلِ اللَّحْمَ وَلَمْ أَبْدُنْ، فَقَالَ لِلنَّاسِ: «تَقَدَّمُوا» فَتَقَدَّمُوا، ثُمَّ قَالَ لِي: «تَعَالَيْ حَتَّى أُسَابِقَكِ» فَسَابَقْتُهُ فَسَبَقْتُهُ، فَسَكَتَ عَنِّي، حَتَّى إِذَا حَمَلْتُ اللَّحْمَ وَبَدُنْتُ وَنَسِيتُ، خَرَجْتُ مَعَهُ فِي بَعْضِ أَسْفَارِهِ، فَقَالَ لِلنَّاسِ: «تَقَدَّمُوا» فَتَقَدَّمُوا، ثُمَّ قَالَ: «تَعَالَيْ حَتَّى أُسَابِقَكِ» فَسَابَقْتُهُ، فَسَبَقَنِي، فَجَعَلَ يَضْحَكُ، وَهُوَ يَقُولُ: «هَذِهِ بِتِلْكَ»

'Aishah said, "I accompanied the Prophet on a journey. At that time, I was a small girl and was neither fat nor bulky. The Prophet asked the people to move on, and they did so. Then the Prophet said, 'Come, let us race.' So I raced him and won. The Prophet kept quiet for some time. Later, when I grew

---

[1] Related by Abu Dawud in his *Sunan* (no. 2214). It is authenticated by Al-Albani is *Al-Sahihah* (no. 131).

78

heavier and had forgotten the previous incident, I accompanied the Prophet on another journey. The Prophet again asked the people to proceed ahead, and they did so. The Prophet again asked me to race him. This time, the Prophet won. He laughed and said, 'This is [payback] for the last time [you beat me].'"[1]

[1] Related by Ahmad in *Al-Musnad* (no. 27548). It was authenticated by Al-Albani in *Silsilah Al-Ahadith Al-Sahihah* (no. 131).

Hadith Thirteen: "O Father of the Dust!"

عَنْ سَهْلِ بْنِ سَعْدٍ، قَالَ: مَا كَانَ لِعَلِيٍّ اسْمٌ أَحَبَّ إِلَيْهِ مِنْ أَبِي تُرَابٍ، وَإِنْ كَانَ
لَيَفْرَحُ بِهِ إِذَا دُعِيَ بِهَا، جَاءَ رَسُولُ اللهِ صَلَّى اللهُ عَلَيْهِ وَسَلَّمَ بَيْتَ فَاطِمَةَ عَلَيْهَا
السَّلَامُ، فَلَمْ يَجِدْ عَلِيًّا فِي البَيْتِ، فَقَالَ: «أَيْنَ ابْنُ عَمِّكِ» فَقَالَتْ: كَانَ بَيْنِي وَبَيْنَهُ
شَيْءٌ، فَغَاضَبَنِي فَخَرَجَ فَلَمْ يَقِلْ عِنْدِي، فَقَالَ رَسُولُ اللهِ صَلَّى اللهُ عَلَيْهِ وَسَلَّمَ
لِإِنْسَانٍ: «انْظُرْ أَيْنَ هُوَ» فَجَاءَ فَقَالَ: يَا رَسُولَ اللهِ هُوَ فِي المَسْجِدِ رَاقِدٌ، فَجَاءَ
رَسُولُ اللهِ صَلَّى اللهُ عَلَيْهِ وَسَلَّمَ وَهُوَ مُضْطَجِعٌ، قَدْ سَقَطَ رِدَاؤُهُ عَنْ شِقِّهِ فَأَصَابَهُ
تُرَابٌ، فَجَعَلَ رَسُولُ اللهِ صَلَّى اللهُ عَلَيْهِ وَسَلَّمَ يَمْسَحُهُ عَنْهُ وَهُوَ يَقُولُ: «قُمْ أَبَا
تُرَابٍ، قُمْ أَبَا تُرَابٍ»

Sahl b. Sa'd reported, "There was no name dearer to 'Ali than his nickname Abu Turab (father of dust). He became happy whenever someone called him by it. Once, the Messenger of Allah came to Fatimah's house but did not find 'Ali at home. So, he asked, 'Where is your cousin?' She replied, 'We quarreled, and he became angry and left without taking his midday nap at my house.' Allah's Messenger asked a person to look for him. That person came and said, 'O Allah's Messenger, he is sleeping in the mosque.' So the Prophet went there and found him lying down. His upper garment had fallen off to one side, and he was covered with dust. Allah's Messenger started cleaning the dust from him, saying, 'Get up, O Abu Turab! Get up, O Abu Turab!'"[1]

---

[1] Related by Al-Bukhari in his *Sahih* (no. 5929) and Muslim in his *Sahih* (no. 4404). A *kunyah* (كُنْيَة) is a by-name that refers to a person as the parent of their eldest son or daughter. It is formed by prefixing "Abu" (بو), meaning "father of," or "Umm" (م), meaning "mother of," to the name of the child. Here, the Prophet صَلَّى اللهُ عَلَيْهِ وَعَلَى آلِهِ وَسَلَّمَ is using it humorously.

80

Hadith Fourteen: "Go and Feed Your Family with It"

عَنْ أَبِي هُرَيْرَةَ رَضِيَ اللهُ عَنْهُ، قَالَ: جَاءَ رَجُلٌ إِلَى النَّبِيِّ صَلَّى اللهُ عَلَيْهِ وَسَلَّمَ، فَقَالَ: هَلَكْتُ، يَا رَسُولَ اللهِ، قَالَ: «وَمَا أَهْلَكَكَ؟» قَالَ: وَقَعْتُ عَلَى امْرَأَتِي فِي رَمَضَانَ، قَالَ: «هَلْ تَجِدُ مَا تُعْتِقُ رَقَبَةً؟» قَالَ: لَا، قَالَ: «فَهَلْ تَسْتَطِيعُ أَنْ تَصُومَ شَهْرَيْنِ مُتَتَابِعَيْنِ؟» قَالَ: لَا، قَالَ: «فَهَلْ تَجِدُ مَا تُطْعِمُ سِتِّينَ مِسْكِينًا؟» قَالَ: لَا، قَالَ: ثُمَّ جَلَسَ، فَأُتِيَ النَّبِيُّ صَلَّى اللهُ عَلَيْهِ وَسَلَّمَ بِعَرَقٍ فِيهِ تَمْرٌ، فَقَالَ: «تَصَدَّقْ بِهَذَا» قَالَ: أَفْقَرَ مِنَّا؟ فَمَا بَيْنَ لَابَتَيْهَا أَهْلُ بَيْتٍ أَحْوَجُ إِلَيْهِ مِنَّا، فَضَحِكَ النَّبِيُّ صَلَّى اللهُ عَلَيْهِ وَسَلَّمَ حَتَّى بَدَتْ أَنْيَابُهُ، ثُمَّ قَالَ: «اذْهَبْ فَأَطْعِمْهُ أَهْلَكَ»

Abu Hurayrah said, "A man came to the Prophet and said, 'O Messenger of Allah, I am destroyed.' The Prophet said, 'What has destroyed you?'

'I had relations with my wife during [the daylight of] *Ramadan*,' he said.

'Are you able to emancipate a slave?' the Messenger of Allah asked.

'No,' he replied.

'Are you able to fast for two consecutive months?'

'No, I am not."

'Are you able to feed sixty poor people?'

'No,' he replied.

He (i.e., the man) then sat down. By and by, someone came to the Messenger of Allah ﷺ with a huge basket of dates. He said to the man, 'Go and give this out in charity (i.e., as an expiation for the sin).'

'O Messenger of Allah, am I to give it to someone poorer than me? There is no family poorer than mine between the two lava fields.'[1]

The Messenger of Allah ﷺ then laughed, showing his molars, and said, 'Go and feed your family with it.'"[2]

---

[1] I.e., Al-Madinah
[2] Related by Muslim in his *Sahih* (no. 1862), Al-Tirmidhi in his *Jami'* (no. 2994) and Ibn Majah in his *Sunan* (no. 1660).

Hadith Fifteen: "May Allah Keep You Smiling"

عَنْ مُحَمَّدِ بْنِ سَعْدِ بْنِ أَبِي وَقَّاصٍ، عَنْ أَبِيهِ، قَالَ: اسْتَأْذَنَ عُمَرُ بْنُ الْخَطَّابِ عَلَى
رَسُولِ اللهِ صَلَّى اللهُ عَلَيْهِ وَسَلَّمَ، وَعِنْدَهُ نِسْوَةٌ مِنْ قُرَيْشٍ يُكَلِّمْنَهُ وَيَسْتَكْثِرْنَهُ، عَالِيَة
أَصْوَاتُهُنَّ عَلَى صَوْتِهِ، فَلَمَّا اسْتَأْذَنَ عُمَرُ بْنُ الْخَطَّابِ قُمْنَ فَبَادَرْنَ الحِجَابَ، فَأَذِنَ
لَهُ رَسُولُ اللهِ صَلَّى اللهُ عَلَيْهِ وَسَلَّمَ فَدَخَلَ عُمَرُ وَرَسُولُ اللهِ صَلَّى اللهُ عَلَيْهِ وَسَلَّمَ
يَضْحَكُ، فَقَالَ عُمَرُ: أَضْحَكَ اللهُ سِنَّكَ يَا رَسُولَ اللهِ، فَقَالَ النَّبِيُّ صَلَّى اللهُ عَلَيْهِ
وَسَلَّمَ: «عَجِبْتُ مِنْ هَؤُلَاءِ اللَّاتِي كُنَّ عِنْدِي، فَلَمَّا سَمِعْنَ صَوْتَكَ ابْتَدَرْنَ
الحِجَابَ» فَقَالَ عُمَرُ: فَأَنْتَ أَحَقُّ أَنْ يَهَبْنَ يَا رَسُولَ اللهِ، ثُمَّ قَالَ عُمَرُ: يَا عَدُوَّاتِ
أَنْفُسِهِنَّ أَتَهَبْنَنِي وَلَا تَهَبْنَ رَسُولَ اللهِ صَلَّى اللهُ عَلَيْهِ وَسَلَّمَ؟ فَقُلْنَ: نَعَمْ، أَنْتَ أَفَظُّ
وَأَغْلَظُ مِنْ رَسُولِ اللهِ صَلَّى اللهُ عَلَيْهِ وَسَلَّمَ، فَقَالَ رَسُولُ اللهِ صَلَّى اللهُ عَلَيْهِ وَسَلَّمَ:
«إِيهًا يَا ابْنَ الْخَطَّابِ، وَالَّذِي نَفْسِي بِيَدِهِ مَا لَقِيَكَ الشَّيْطَانُ سَالِكًا فَجًّا قَطُّ، إِلَّا
سَلَكَ فَجًّا غَيْرَ فَجِّكَ»

Sa'd b. Abu Waqqas said, "'Umar b. Al-Khattab sought permission to enter upon the Messenger of Allah while some Quraysh women sat with him and asked him for help. They were raising their voices above his. When 'Umar asked to enter, they hurried to veil themselves. The Prophet allowed 'Umar to enter, and he (i.e., the Prophet) was laughing. 'Umar said, 'May Allah keep you smiling, O Messenger of Allah.' The Prophet said, 'I am amazed by these women who were with me. As soon as they heard your voice, they rushed to cover themselves.' 'Umar said, 'You have more right that they should be modest in front of you, O Messenger of Allah.' Then Umar turned to them and said, 'O enemies of your own souls! You are modest for me but not for the Messenger of Allah?' The women replied, 'Yes, because you are stricter and harsher than him.' The Prophet said, 'O son of Khattab, by the One in Whose Hand is my soul, whenever *Shaytan* sees you taking a path, he takes another one.'"[1]

'Umar's statement, "May Allah keep you smiling," means "May Allah maintain your happiness and joy."[2]

---

[1] Collected by Al-Bukhari in his *Sahih* (no. 3294) and Muslim (no. 2396).
[2] Refer to *'Awn Al-Ma'bud* (14/99)

Hadith Sixteen: "Smear Her Face"

قَالَتْ عَائِشَةُ: أَتَيْتُ النَّبِيَّ صَلَّى اللهُ عَلَيْهِ وَسَلَّمَ بِخَزِيرَةٍ قَدْ طَبَخْتُهَا لَهُ، فَقُلْتُ لِسَوْدَةَ
. وَالنَّبِيُّ صَلَّى اللهُ عَلَيْهِ وَسَلَّمَ بَيْنِي وَبَيْنَهَا: كُلِي، فَأَبَتْ، فَقُلْتُ: لَتَأْكُلِنَّ أَوْ لَأُلَطِّخَنَّ
وَجْهَكِ، فَأَبَتْ، فَوَضَعْتُ يَدِي فِي الْخَزِيرَةِ، فَطَلَيْتُ وَجْهَهَا، فَضَحِكَ النَّبِيُّ صَلَّى اللهُ
عَلَيْهِ وَسَلَّمَ، فَوَضَعَ بِيَدِهِ لَهَا، وَقَالَ لَهَا: «الْطَخِي وَجْهَهَا»، فَضَحِكَ النَّبِيُّ صَلَّى اللهُ
عَلَيْهِ وَسَلَّمَ

'Aishah said, "I came to the Prophet with a dish of *khazirah*[1] I prepared for him. While the Prophet was between us, I said to Sawdah, 'Eat some.' She refused. So, I responded, 'I swear, you will either eat it, or I will rub it on your face!' She still refused, so I put my hand in the *khazirah* and wiped her face. The Prophet laughed, gave Sawdah his hand, and said, 'Smear her face.' Sawdah did so, and the Prophet again laughed."[2]

While critics of polygyny often cite instances of jealousy among co-wives, this narration shows a lighthearted interaction between the Prophet ﷺ and the Mothers of the Believers. It also illustrates the importance of humor and playfulness within such relationships.

---

[1] A meal made from chunks of meat, fat, and flour, cooked with water until it reaches the consistency of thick gravy. Refer to *Fath Al-Bari* (9/454).
[2] Collected by Abu Ya'la Al-Musali in his *Musnad* (7/449). It has been authenticated by Al-Albani in *Silsilah Al-Ahadith Al-Sahihah* (no. 3131).

Hadith Seventeen: The Fragile Vessels

عَنْ أَنَسِ بْنِ مَالِكٍ قَالَ: أَتَى النَّبِيُّ صَلَّى الله عَلَيْهِ وَسَلَّم عَلَى بَعْضِ نِسَائِهِ – وَمَعُهُنَّ أُمُّ سُلَيْمٍ – فَقَالَ: يَا أَنْجَشَةُ، رُوَيْدًا سَوْقَكَ بِالْقَوَارِيرِ «قَالَ أَبُو قِلَابَةَ: فَتَكَلَّمَ النَّبِيُّ صَلَّى الله عَلَيْهِ وَسَلَّم بِكَلِمَةٍ لَوْ تَكَلَّمَ بِهَا بَعْضُكُمْ لَعِبْتُمُوهَا عَلَيْهِ، قَوْلُهُ: سَوْقَكَ بِالْقَوَارِيرِ»

Anas b. Malik reported, "[While on a journey], the Prophet came to some of his wives, and Umm Sulaym was with them. He said, 'O Anjashah![1] Be gentle when driving the camels carrying fragile vessels.'"

Abu Qilabah said, "The Prophet used words that, if spoken by one of you, would have been criticized. He said, 'Be gentle when driving the camels carrying fragile vessels.'"[2]

Al-Bukhari collects this in "The Chapter of Joking," indicating that the Prophet ﷺ humorously said this.

This is an example of permissible joking because women *are* physically fragile. *Al-Hafiz* Al-Nawawi said, "The scholars say women are called "*qawarir*" (glass vessels) because they are delicate and can break easily, like glass."[3]

---

[1] Anjashah was a companion of the Prophet. He was known for his beautiful voice and was responsible for leading the women's camels during journeys. Refer to *Sahih Al-Adab Al-Mufrad* (p. 116).

[2] Collected Al-Bukhari in *Al-Adab Al-Mufrad* (no. 264) in "The Chapter of Joking." Authenticated by Al-Albani in *Sahih Al-Adab Al-Mufrad* (no. 199).

[3] *Sharh Sahih Muslim* (15/474)

Appendix I: A Glimpse at the Humor of the Companions

"Faith in Their Hearts Was Greater Than a Mountain"

Someone asked Ibn 'Umar, "Did the companions of the Messenger of Allah laugh?" He answered, "Yes, and *Iman* (faith) in their hearts was greater than a mountain."[1]

وعن سُفيانَ بنِ محمد، قال: كان ابنُ عُمَر من أفوحِ النَّاسِ وأضحَكِهم.

Sufyan b. Muhammad said, "Ibn 'Umar was one of the most humorous and amusing people."[2]

Nafi' reported that 'Abd Allah b. 'Umar used to joke with his maidservant by saying to her, "The Creator of the noble created me, and the Creator of the ignoble created you." She would get angry and shout, and 'Abd Allah would laugh.[3]

One must reconcile this with Ibn 'Umar's strict adherence to the Prophet's *Sunnah*. It is reported that he used to follow the commands and traditions of the Messenger of Allah ﷺ with such concern that some feared for his sanity.[4] He was firm upon the *Sunnah* yet still engaged in humor. This balance defined him.

---

[1] Refer to the *Tafsir Al-Baghawi* (7/418).
[2] *Mudarah Al-Nas* (p. 64)
[3] *Akhbar Al-Ziraf wa Al-Mutamajinin* (p. 57)
[4] Refer to *Siyar A'lam Al-Nubala* (3/212).

"He Used to Make the Messenger of Allah Laugh"

عَنْ عُمَرَ بْنِ الخَطَّابِ، أَنَّ رَجُلًا عَلَى عَهْدِ النَّبِيِّ صَلَّى اللهُ عَلَيْهِ وَسَلَّمَ كَانَ اسْمُهُ عَبْدَ اللهِ، وَكَانَ يُلَقَّبُ حِمَارًا، وَكَانَ يُضْحِكُ رَسُولَ اللهِ صَلَّى اللهُ عَلَيْهِ وَسَلَّمَ، وَكَانَ النَّبِيُّ صَلَّى اللهُ عَلَيْهِ وَسَلَّمَ قَدْ جَلَدَهُ فِي الشَّرَابِ، فَأُتِيَ بِهِ يَوْمًا فَأَمَرَ بِهِ فَجُلِدَ، فَقَالَ رَجُلٌ مِنَ الْقَوْمِ: اللَّهُمَّ الْعَنْهُ، مَا أَكْثَرَ مَا يُؤْتَى بِهِ؟ فَقَالَ النَّبِيُّ صَلَّى اللهُ عَلَيْهِ وَسَلَّمَ: «لَا تَلْعَنُوهُ، فَوَاللهِ مَا عَلِمْتُ إِنَّهُ يُحِبُّ اللهَ وَرَسُولَهُ»

'Umar b. Al-Khattab reported, "During the lifetime of the Prophet, there was a man named 'Abd Allah, nicknamed *Himar* (donkey), who used to make the Messenger of Allah ﷺ laugh. The Prophet lashed him for drinking [intoxicants]. One day, he was brought to the Prophet for the same offense and lashed again. Someone said, 'O Allah, curse him! How frequently he has been brought [to the Prophet for such an offense]!' The Prophet said: 'Do not curse him, for by Allah, I know he loves Allah and His Messenger.'"[1]

Regarding this narration, Ibn Hajr says, "His statement, 'He used to make the Prophet laugh,' means he used to do things to amuse him. Abu Ya'la collects Hisham b. Sa'd's narration from Zayd b. Aslam that a man nicknamed *Himar* sent a gift of honey or fat to the Messenger of Allah. When the seller came to collect the price, [*Himar*] took him to the Messenger of Allah to pay for it. This made the Prophet laugh. He then had someone pay the seller."[2]

---

[1] Collected by Al-Bukhari in his *Sahih* (no. 6398).
[2] *Fath Al-Bari* (12/77)

"You Resemble the Prophet"

عَنْ عُقْبَةَ بْنِ الحَارِثِ، قَالَ: رَأَيْتُ أَبَا بَكْرٍ رَضِيَ اللَّهُ عَنْهُ، وَحَمَلَ الحَسَنَ وَهُوَ يَقُولُ:
«بِأَبِي شَبِيهٌ بِالنَّبِيِّ، لَيْسَ شَبِيهٌ بِعَلِيٍّ» وَعَلِيٌّ يَضْحَكُ

'Uqbah b. Al-Harith reported, "I saw Abu Bakr carrying Al-Hasan and saying, 'Let my father be sacrificed for you. You resemble the Prophet, not Ali,' and Ali was laughing [at this]."[1]

Ibn Hajr said, "In the narration of Al-Isma'ili, he says, 'And 'Ali smiled,' indicating acceptance and approval of Abu Bakr's words [...] The narration illustrates the virtue of Abu Bakr and his love for the Prophet's kinship. It also highlights the permissibility of allowing even distinguished children to play, as Al-Hasan was seven years old and had heard and memorized [traditions] from the Prophet. His play was appropriate for his age, contributing to his exercise and well-being. Allah knows best."[2]

---

[1] This is collected by Al-Bukhari in his *Sahih* (no. 3750).
[2] *Fath Al-Bari* (6/652)

"Do Not Kill Yourselves"

عَنْ عَمْرِو بْنِ الْعَاصِ قَالَ: احْتَلَمْتُ فِي لَيْلَةٍ بَارِدَةٍ فِي غَزْوَةٍ ذَاتِ السُّلَاسِلِ
فَأَشْفَقْتُ إِنِ اغْتَسَلْتُ أَنْ أَهْلِكَ فَتَيَمَّمْتُ، ثُمَّ صَلَّيْتُ بِأَصْحَابِي الصُّبْحَ فَذَكَرُوا
ذَلِكَ لِلنَّبِيِّ صَلَّى اللهُ عَلَيْهِ وَسَلَّمَ فَقَالَ: «يَا عَمْرُو صَلَّيْتَ بِأَصْحَابِكَ وَأَنْتَ
جُنُبٌ؟» فَأَخْبَرْتُهُ بِالَّذِي مَنَعَنِي مِنَ الِاغْتِسَالِ وَقُلْتُ إِنِّي سَمِعْتُ اللهَ يَقُولُ: {وَلَا
تَقْتُلُوا أَنْفُسَكُمْ إِنَّ اللهَ كَانَ بِكُمْ رَحِيمًا} [النساء: 29] فَضَحِكَ رَسُولُ اللهِ صَلَّى
اللهُ عَلَيْهِ وَسَلَّمَ وَلَمْ يَقُلْ شَيْئًا

'Amr b. Al-'As said, "I had a wet dream on a cold night during the battle of *Dhat Al-Salasil*. I was afraid that if I performed *ghusl*, I would die. I, therefore, performed *tayammum* and led my companions in the morning prayer. They mentioned this to the Messenger of Allah ﷺ. He said, "Amr, you led your companions in prayer while you were in a state of sexual impurity?' I informed him of what prevented me from taking a bath. I said, I heard Allah say,

$$\{ وَلَا تَقْتُلُوٓا۟ أَنفُسَكُمْ ۚ إِنَّ ٱللَّهَ كَانَ بِكُمْ رَحِيمًا \}$$

'Do not kill yourselves, verily Allah is Merciful to you.'
[*Al-Nisa* 4:29]

The Messenger of Allah ﷺ laughed and said nothing."[1]

Concerning his statement, "The Messenger of Allah laughed and said nothing," Al-Azim Abadi said, "This is evidence for the permissibility of performing *tayammum* in severe cold from

---

[1] Collected by Abu Dawud in his *Sunan* (no. 334). It has been authenticated by Al-Albani in *Sahih Abu Dawud* (no. 334).

two aspects: The first is his laughing, and the second is his not objecting because the Prophet ﷺ does not approve of falsehood. Thus, his laughter shows approval more than remaining silent."[1]

---

[1] *Awn Al-Ma'bud* (1/365)

"A Horse with Two Wings?"

عَنْ عَائِشَةَ رَضِيَ اللَّهُ عَنْهَا، قَالَتْ: قَدِمَ رَسُولُ اللَّهِ صَلَّى اللَّهُ عَلَيْهِ وَسَلَّمَ مِنْ غَزْوَةِ
تَبُوكَ، أَوْ خَيْبَرَ وَفِي سَهْوَتِهَا سِتْرٌ، فَهَبَّتْ رِيحٌ فَكَشَفَتْ نَاحِيةَ السِّتْرِ عَنْ بَنَاتٍ
لِعَائِشَةَ لُعَبٍ، فَقَالَ: «مَا هَذَا يَا عَائِشَةُ؟» قَالَتْ: بَنَاتِي، وَرَأَى بَيْنَهُنَّ فَرَسًا لَهُ
جَنَاحَانِ مِنْ رِقَاعٍ، فَقَالَ: «مَا هَذَا الَّذِي أَرَى وَسْطَهُنَّ؟» قَالَتْ: فَرَسٌ، قَالَ:
«وَمَا هَذَا الَّذِي عَلَيْهِ؟» قَالَتْ: جَنَاحَانِ، قَالَ: «فَرَسٌ لَهُ جَنَاحَانِ؟» قَالَتْ: أَمَا
سَمِعْتَ أَنَّ لِسُلَيْمَانَ خَيْلًا لَهَا أَجْنِحَةٌ؟ قَالَتْ: فَضَحِكَ حَتَّى رَأَيْتُ نَوَاجِذَهُ

'Aishah reported that when the Messenger of Allah returned
from the Tabuk or Khaybar expedition, a breeze raised the end
of a curtain in front of her room, revealing some of her dolls.

"What is this, O 'Aishah?" he asked.

"My dolls," she replied.

He saw a horse with wings made of rags and asked, "What is
this I see among them?"

"A horse," she said.

"What is this that it has on it?"

"Two wings."

"A horse with two wings?" he said.

"Have you not heard that Sulayman had horses with wings?"

The Prophet laughed until I could see his molar teeth.[1]

---

[1] Collected by Abu Dawud in his *Sunan* (no. 4932). It has been authenticated
by Al-Albani in *Sahih Abu Dawud* (no. 4932).

"This Is What I Wanted"

عَنْ عَبْدِ الرَّحْمَنِ بْنِ أَبِي لَيْلَى، عَنْ أُسَيْدِ بْنِ حُضَيْرٍ، رَجُلٍ مِنَ الْأَنْصَارِ قَالَ: بَيْنَمَا
هُوَ يُحَدِّثُ الْقَوْمَ وَكَانَ فِيهِ مِزَاحٌ بَيْنَا يُضْحِكُهُمْ فَطَعَنَهُ النَّبِيُّ صَلَّى اللهُ عَلَيْهِ وَسَلَّمَ فِي
خَاصِرَتِهِ بِعُودٍ فَقَالَ: أَصْبِرْنِي فَقَالَ: «اصْطَبِرْ» قَالَ: إِنَّ عَلَيْكَ قَمِيصًا وَلَيْسَ عَلَيَّ
قَمِيصٌ، «فَرَفَعَ النَّبِيُّ صَلَّى اللهُ عَلَيْهِ وَسَلَّمَ عَنْ قَمِيصِهِ، فَاحْتَضَنَهُ وَجَعَلَ يُقَبِّلُ
كَشْحَهُ»، قَالَ إِنَّمَا أَرَدْتُ هَذَا يَا رَسُولَ اللهِ

'Abd Al-Rahman b. Abu Layla related from Usayd b. Hudayr, a man of the Ansar, that while he was talking to the people, jesting with them, and making them laugh, the Prophet poked him in the ribs with a stick.

"Let me retaliate," he said.

"Retaliate," the Prophet said.

"You are wearing a shirt, but I am not."

The Prophet then raised his shirt, and the man embraced him and kissed his side. He said, "This is what I wanted, O Messenger of Allah!"[1]

---

[1] Collected by Abu Dawud in his *Sunan* (no. 5224). Al-Albani said, "It has a *Sahih* chain of narration. See *Sahih Abu Dawud* (no. 5224).

93

"He Is Either From Quraysh or the Ansar"

وعن أبي هُرَيْرَةَ رَضِيَ الله عنه: أَنَّ النَّبِيَّ صَلَّى الله عليه وسَلَّم كان يوماً يُحَدِّثُ وعنده رجُلٌ من أهلِ البادِيةِ، أَنَّ رجُلًا من أهلِ الجَنَّةِ استأذن رَبَّه في الزَّرع، فقال له: ألَسْتَ فيما شِئْتَ؟ !قال: بلى، ولكِنِّي أُحِبُّ أن أَزْرَعَ !قال: فَبَذَر، دُوَنَك يا ابَنَ آدَمَ؛ فإنَّه لا يُشبِعُك شيءٌ !فقال الأعرابِيُّ: والله لا تَجِدُه إلَّا قُرَشِيًّا أو أنصارِيًّا؛ فإنَّهم أصحابُ زَرع، وأمَّا نحنُ فلَسْنا بأصحابِ زَرع !فضَحِك النَّبِيُّ صَلَّى الله عليه وسَلَّم

Abu Hurayrah reported the Prophet was speaking while a Bedouin was present. The Prophet said, "A man from the people of Paradise asked Allah to allow him to cultivate the land. Allah said to him, 'Don't you have whatever you desire?' He replied, 'Yes, but I enjoy cultivating the land.' So, he sowed the seeds, and the plants multiplied and were harvested, resembling mountains. Allah then said [to him], 'Here you are, O son of Adam, for nothing satisfies you.'"

The Bedouin said, "O Allah's Messenger, such a man must be from Quraysh or the Ansar, for they are farmers, but we are not." At this, Allah's Messenger laughed.[1]

---

[1] Collected by Al-Bukhari in his *Sahih* (no. 2348).

"All of Me or Part of Me?"

قال عَوْف بْن مَالِكٍ أتيتُ النبيَّ صلَّى اللهُ عليه وسلم وهو في بناءٍ له من أدمٍ فسلمتُ عليه فقال لي : يا عوفُ ، قلتُ : نعم ، قال لي : ادخلْ ، قلتُ : كلِّي أو بعضي ؟ قال : بل كلّك.

'Awf b. Malik said, "I came to the Prophet while he was in a tent made of leather and greeted him.

"O 'Awf," he said.

"Yes," I replied.

"Enter."

"All of me or part of me?" I said.

"All of you."[1]

'Uthman b. Abu Al-Atikah mentioned that 'Awf said, '[Part of me or] all of me?' because of the small size of the tent.[2]

This narration shows that even during the difficulties and hardships of the Tabuk Expedition, the Prophet ﷺ did not object to his companion's use of humor.

---

[1] Authenticated by Al-Albani in *Takhrij Fada'il Al-Sham wa Al-Dimashq* (p. 67)

[2] Refer to *Fath Al-Bari* (6/278).

Appendix II: A Glimpse at the Humor of the Scholars

Some critics insist that the people of *Sunnah* are always strict and austere. While strict adherence to the *Sunnah* is praiseworthy, humor and laughter do not contradict it when following the Prophet's guidance. These qualities are inherent in the children of Adam and were exhibited by the Messenger of Allah ﷺ and his noble companions.

Therefore, it is beneficial to highlight a few instances where the scholars of the *Sunnah*—past and present—engaged in humor. It is also important to note that they always stayed within the limits prescribed by Islamic teachings, maintaining truthfulness and dignity. These examples are not exhaustive, as those who attended their lessons or accompanied them witnessed their humor in different situations. May Allah, the source of joy and laughter, bestow His Mercy upon them and elevate them to the highest ranks of Paradise.

Al-Imam Muhammad b. Sirin

Yunus said, "Muhammad b. Sirin was known for his laughter and good humor."[1]

It is reported that Ibn Sirin used to play around and laugh until he would drool, but when you asked him about something related to his religion, he would become serious.[2]

Once, someone told Ibn Sirin, "Whoever eats seven dates on an empty stomach, the dates will glorify Allah (*tasbih*)!" Ibn Sirin replied, "If that is the case, then an almond should pray *tarawih* and *witr* if eaten."[3]

Ghalib al-Qattan said, "I went to Ibn Sirin one day and asked about Hisham. He replied, 'He passed away yesterday, didn't you know?' I said, 'To Allah, we belong, and to Him we shall return.' Then he laughed." Al-Baghawi added, "Perhaps he meant he went to sleep."[4]

This alludes to the old saying, "Sleep is the brother of death," based on the Prophet's ﷺ statement:

النومُ أخو الموتِ ، ولا يموتُ أهلُ الجنَّةِ

"Sleep is death's brother, and the people of Paradise do not die."[5]

---

[1] *Mudarat Al-Nas* (p. 67)

[2] Refer to *Sharh Al-Sunnah* by Al-Baghawi (13/184).

[3] *Bahjah Al-Majalis* (1/101)

[4] *Sharh Al-Sunnah* (13/184)

[5] Refer to *Sahih Al-Jami'* of Al-Albani (no. 6808).

Al-Imam Al-Sha'bi

Al-A'mash said, "A man came to Al-Sha'bi and said, 'What is Iblis's wife's name?' Al-Sha'bi replied, 'I did not attend that wedding.'"[1]

Al-Sha'bi's reply suggests that the question was irrelevant and that he had no interest in pursuing it.

The classical scholars of *tafsir* relate this narration in their commentary on Allah's statement:

﴿ وَإِذْ قُلْنَا لِلْمَلَٰئِكَةِ ٱسْجُدُوا۟ لِءَادَمَ فَسَجَدُوٓا۟ إِلَّآ إِبْلِيسَ كَانَ مِنَ ٱلْجِنِّ فَفَسَقَ عَنْ أَمْرِ رَبِّهِۦٓ أَفَتَتَّخِذُونَهُۥ وَذُرِّيَّتَهُۥٓ أَوْلِيَآءَ مِن دُونِى وَهُمْ لَكُمْ عَدُوٌّۢ بِئْسَ لِلظَّٰلِمِينَ بَدَلًا ﴾

And (remember) when We said to the angels, "Prostrate to Adam." So they prostrated except Iblis (Satan). He was one of the *jinns*. He disobeyed the Command of his Lord. Will you then take him (Iblis) and his offspring as protectors and helpers rather than Me while they are enemies to you? What an evil is the exchange for the *zalimun* (polytheists, and wrong-doers, *et cetera*)" (*Al-Kahf* 18:50).

For example, Al-Baghawi cites al-Sha'bi's statement, "I was sitting one day when a man approached me and asked, 'Tell me, does *Shaytan* have a wife?' I replied, 'That is a wedding I did not attend!' Then I remembered Allah's statement: 'Do you

---

[1] *Al-Ma'rifah wa Al-Tarikh* (2/603)

take him and his descendants as allies besides Me?' I realized descendants can only come from a wife, so I said, 'Yes.'"[1]

Finally, it is reported that a man asked al-Sha'bi about wiping his beard during ablution, and he said, "Run your fingers through it."

"I'm afraid it won't get wet," the man said.

"Then start soaking it at the beginning of the night," Al-Sha'bi said.[2]

---

[1] *Tafsir Al-Baghawi* (3/198)
Qatadah said, "They reproduce just as the children of Adam do." Refer to *Tafsir Al-Baghawi* (3/198).
[2] *Akhbar Al-Ziraf wa Al-Mutamajin* (p. 62)

Al-Qadi Abu Tayyib al-Tabari

Abu Ishaq Al-Shirazi said, "Al-Qadi Abu Tayyib Al-Tabari gave a shoe to a cobbler for repair. He would pass by the cobbler to get it, but every time the cobbler saw him, he would take the shoe and dip it in water, saying, 'It will be ready soon!' When Al-Qadi grew impatient, he said, 'I gave you this shoe to repair it, not to teach it how to swim.'"[1]

---

[1] *Al-Muntazam* (8/198)

Al-Imam Ibrahim b. Adham

Abu 'Abd Al-Rahman Al-A'raj said, "Ibrahim b. Adham used to narrate to us and make us laugh."[1]

'Isa b. Khazim Al-Naysaburi said, "We were in Makkah with Ibrahim b. Adham, and he looked at Abu Qubays and said, 'If a believer, complete in his faith, were to shake a mountain, it would move.' Abu Qubays trembled. So, he said, 'Be still, I did not mean you.'"[2]

---

[1] *Rawdah Al-'Uqala* (p. 81)
[2] *Siyar 'Alam Al-Nubala* (7/388)

Shaykh Muhammad b. Ibrahim Ali Al-Shaykh

'Abd Al-'Aziz b. Shalhub, renowned for his excellent recitation and beautiful voice, made a single mistake while reading: (وهذه لُغَةُ حِمْيَرٍ) "And this is the language of Himyar."[1] He read it as (وهذه لُغَةُ حَمِيرٍ), "And this is the language of donkeys." So, *Shaykh* Muhammad b. Ibrahim said, "*Subhanallah*, do donkeys have a language?"[2]

---

[1] I.e., the Himyarite people.
[2] *Irtisamat* (p. 56)

Shaykh 'Abd Allah Al-Qar'awi

Shaykh Muhammad Shayban recalled one trip he and another student, Ahmad Ibrahim, took with *Shaykh* Al-Qar'awi. They were traveling to the mountain of Fayfa to deliver school supplies: notebooks, clothes, and charity to *Shaykh* Muhammad Al-Qarni's school. This was in the winter. They set out from Bisha, stopping in the village of 'Akwah after 'Isha. A group of Bedouins hosted them generously. At night, the *Shaykh* covered his two students with his wool cloak to protect them from the cold. The next morning, they continued their travels. The *Shaykh* walked while the students rode his donkey. "We were young," *Shaykh* Muhammad Shayban said.

When they arrived at the village of Balghazi, they dismounted at the house of Al-Qadi 'Abd Allah b. Musa. The people of Balghazi were known for their coffee, and the Qadi poured some for *Shaykh* 'Abd Allah, who enjoyed it immensely, drinking several cups. "I have not tasted coffee like this in some time," he said. After eating lunch and purchasing some necessary items, they moved on. As they began climbing the Fayfa mountain, the *Shaykh* feared the students might fall, so he strapped them to the donkey. They arrived at their destination that evening. The students' hands had cracked from the bitter cold. The *Shaykh* instructed them to help *Shaykh* Muhammad Al-Qarni teach his students.

Meanwhile, he distributed the school supplies and charity, then departed. On his return, highway robbers confronted him, but Allah delivered him safely, and he joined a traveling caravan. *Shaykh* Muhammad Shayban said, "We stayed [in Fayfa] until the *Shaykh* allowed us to return home. When we saw him, we said, 'Look at our hands, *Shaykh*.' They were cracked from the cold. [We showed him this] so he would not chastise us. Instead, he began to joke with us and laugh: 'May Allah forgive you, my sons!'"[1]

Also, *Shaykh* Ibrahim Al-Sha'bi recounted, "After we ate lunch, we prayed 'Asr, then drove to [*Shaykh* Muhammad b. Ibrahim's] farm. *Shaykh* 'Abd Allah [Al-Qar'awi] joked with *Shaykh* Muhammad, saying, 'Where are we now, *Shaykh* Muhammad?' And he answered, 'We are at such-and-such a place.' He was spot on, even though he was blind. After some time, [*Shaykh* 'Abd Allah] again asked, 'Where are we now?' And *Shaykh* Muhammad again answered correctly. *Shaykh* 'Abd Allah asked, 'How fast is the car going?' *Shaykh* Muhammad correctly answered, 'Such-and-such a speed.' *Shaykh* 'Abd Allah said, 'There is nothing left, *Shaykh* Muhammad, but to have you drive.'"[2]

---

[1] *Al-Nahdah* (pp. 195-196)
[2] *Al-Masirah* (p. 153)

Shaykh 'Abd Al-Rahman Al-Sa'di

Muhammad b. *Shaykh* 'Abd Al-Rahman al-Sa'di said, "The *Shaykh* (i.e., his father) often accepted invitations to have coffee. At the end of Dhu Al-Hijjah one year, a friend invited him, but the *Shaykh* jokingly apologized and said, 'I have many appointments.' His friend insisted and seemed angry at the *Shaykh's* refusal. So, the *Shaykh* said, 'Then your appointment is next year.' His friend became even angrier and said, 'You don't want to come to my house.' The *Shaykh* said, 'My brother, next Tuesday—in two days—is the beginning of the new year. Don't you know we are at the end of this year?' His friend's mood improved when he realized the *Shaykh* was joking with him."[1]

He also related, "My father, may Allah have mercy on him, had a relative named Muhammad Mansur b. Ibrahim Al-Sa'di, who was his close companion. They were born on the same night. Muhammad was born around midnight, while *Shaykh* 'Abd Al-Rahman was born later that morning. So, Muhammad was eight hours older than the *Shaykh*. As they grew older, *Shaykh* 'Abd Al-Rahman's beard turned very white, while Muhammad Mansur's beard was black with a little white. When my father and Muhammad attended gatherings with friends, my father would say, 'Muhammad Mansur has me by eight,' without explaining what he meant by eight. Those in attendance would think that Muhammad was eight *years* older than the *Shaykh*, especially since Muhammad did not speak out of respect for the *Shaykh*, knowing that my father was joking. When

---

[1] *Irtisamat* (p. 49)

attendees expressed amazement, the *Shaykh* would inform them that Muhammad was eight *hours* older than him."[1]

Shaykh Muhammad Nasir Al-Din Al-Albani and Shaykh 'Abd Al-'Aziz Ibn Baz

Once, a student of knowledge was riding with *Shaykh* Al-Albani in his car, and the *Shaykh* was speeding. The student said, "O *Shaykh*, please slow down. *Shaykh* Ibn Baz believes driving fast endangers a person."

Shaykh Al-Albani responded, "This is a *fatwa* from someone who has not driven a car."

"May I inform *Shaykh* Ibn Baz of this?" the student said.

"Yes, inform him."

By and by, the student informed *Shaykh* Ibn Baz of *Shaykh* Al-Albani's statement. He laughed and said, "Tell him that is the *fatwa* of someone who has not yet paid the blood-wit."[1]

---

[1] Refer to *Al-Imam Ibn Baz Durus wa Al-Mawaqif wa Al-'Ibar* (p. 73) by 'Abd Al-'Aziz b. Al-Sadhan.

The blood-wit refers to financial compensation paid to a victim's family or heirs in cases of unintentional or accidental homicide or injury. Here, the *Shaykh* jokingly refers to *Shaykh* Al-Albani paying the blood-wit if he accidentally harms someone by speeding.

Shaykh Muhammad Nasir Al-Din Al-Albani

A questioner asked *Shaykh* Al-Albani, "What is the ruling on lying in jest?"

"What's that?" *Shaykh* Al-Albani said.

"Lying in jest, like using euphemisms, what is its ruling?"

"I don't understand," *Shaykh* Al-Albani said.

"Lying in jest?" another questioner said.

"Yes."

"It's a forgivable lie! (Everyone laughs.) Do you think jesting permits lying?" *Shaykh* Al-Albani said.

"Euphemisms and indirect expressions?" the questioner said.

"Euphemisms and indirect expressions - may Allah bless you - differ from jesting. Lying in jest is perhaps worse than lying...Do you know why? Because the Prophet used to joke, but he only told the truth. So, if someone jokes *and* lies, they are sinning and going against the practice of the Prophet, who joked but always told the truth.

Using euphemisms and indirect expressions is different. If there is a necessity to use them, it is better than outright lying. However, when should one do that? Only when there is a need.

It is also impermissible if someone does so without reason or necessity."[1]

[1] Muhammad Nasir Al-Din Al-Albani, "حكم الكذب في المزاح واستعمال الكناية والمعاريض," accessed June 10, 2024, https://www.al-albany.com/audios/content/141672/.

Shaykh 'Abd Al-'Aziz b. Baz

When *Shaykh* Ibn Baz had guests after 'Isha prayer, he would invite them to stay for dinner. He would tease them if they declined, saying, "Are you afraid of your wife? If not, stay and eat. If so, then excuse yourself."

Once, someone asked a student of knowledge, "Why don't you practice polygamy?"

He replied, "I am a *muwahhid*."

The *Shaykh* responded, "Poor fellow! This is the *tawhid*[1] of the terrified."[2]

Next, *Al-Muhaddith*, *Shaykh* 'Abd Al-Muhsin Al-'Abbad, recounted a humorous remark by *Al-Allamah*, *Shaykh* 'Abd Al-'Aziz b. Baz: *Shaykh* Ibn Baz once joked that while he was staying in Madinah, he traveled to Riyadh and met with *Shaykh* 'Abd Al-'Aziz b. Majid, the *mu'adhin* of the *Al-Jami' Al-Kabir* in Riyadh—may Allah have mercy on him. *Shaykh* Ibn Baz said to him, 'Yesterday, I heard you call the *adhan* thirty minutes early!'"[3]

---

[1] This is a play on words. Linguistically, the verb (وحد) means to make singular. In the Islamic legislation, it refers to singling out Allah alone for worship. Here, the word *"muwahhid"* carries a dual meaning: devotion to Allah alone and fidelity to his wife alone. The *Shaykh's* response plays on this. In other words, this second type of *tawhid*—taking only one wife—is the *tawhid* of the terrified.

[2] Refer to *Al-Imam Ibn Baz Durus wa Al-Mawaqif wa Al-'Ibar* (p. 73) by 'Abd Al-Aziz b. Al-Sadhan.

[3] From the lessons of *Sharh Sunan Abu Dawud*, chapter: "What has been Reported Concerning Joking" by *Shaykh* 'Abd Al-Muhsin Al-Abbad.

The humor comes from the *adhan* being called thirty minutes later in Madinah than in Riyadh. Thus, *Shaykh* Ibn Baz joked about hearing *Shaykh* 'Abd Al-'Aziz's call to prayer on the radio.

Finally, during a gathering, someone mentioned in Ahmad b. Nasr Al-Khuza'i's biography that he performed an exorcism on a possessed man. During the exorcism, a female *jinn* spoke through his tongue and said to Ahmad b. Nasr, "O *Shaykh*, I will not leave this man until he stops saying that the Qur'an is created!"

Shaykh Ibn Baz smiled and said, "*Ma sha Allah*! This is a *Sunni jinn*. She is from the people of *Sunnah*."[1]

---

[1] *Irtisamat* (p. 59)

Shaykh Muhammad b. Salih Al-ʿUthaymin

Once, *Shaykh* Al-ʿUthaymin prayed in the Haram in Makkah, then took a taxi to Mina.

During the trip, the driver wanted to get to know his passenger. "Who is the *shaykh*?" he asked.

"Muhammad b. ʿUthaymin," the *Shaykh* replied.

"You are *Shaykh* Ibn ʿUthaymin?" the driver responded, thinking he was jesting.

"Yes," The *Shaykh* said.

The driver shook his head at his audacity to impersonate *Shaykh* Al-ʿUthaymin. The *Shaykh* asked the driver, "And who is the brother?"

"I am *Shaykh* ʿAbd Al-ʿAziz b. Baz!"

"But Ibn Baz is blind and cannot drive a car."

When the driver realized he was *Shaykh* Al-ʿUthaymin, he apologized, embarrassed.[1]

Next, it is reported that *Shaykh* Muhammad Al-ʿUthaymin said to *Shaykh* ʿAbd Allah Al-Qashʿami, the former *imam* of Al-Thuwayr Mosque, "What is this name? Thuwayr[2]! Couldn't it have been named Thawr?"

---

[1] *Al-Jamiʿ li Hayah Al-Allamah Muhammad b. Salih Al-Uthaymin* (pp. 41-42)
[2] *Thuwayr* is the diminutive form of the word *thawr*, indicating small size.

Shaykh 'Abd Allah replied, "May Allah bless you, *Shaykh* Muhammad. Here in our humble surroundings, this name suits us well. And even the *thuwayr* is powerful. But you are in a city of scholars, nobles, and dignitaries called 'Unayzah.[1] An *'unz* is already small, so what if you make it smaller?"

Shaykh Al-Uthaymin laughed, admiring his quick wit, and remarked, "If I had kept quiet, I would have been safe."[2]

Next, a questioner asked *Shaykh* al-'Uthaymin, "If a person is listening to a recording of the *Qur'an* and hears a verse of prostration, should he prostrate?" The *Shaykh* responded, "Yes, if the recording prostrates."

On another occasion, *Shaykh* al-'Uthaymin taught a lesson on marrying women with physical defects. Someone asked him, "If I married a woman and then found out that she did not have any teeth, does this defect allow me to annul the marriage?" The *Shaykh* responded, "This is a good wife! She cannot bite you."[3]

---

[1] This is the diminutive form of *'unz*.

[2] *Irtisamat* (p. 60)

[3] Muhammad Al-Uthaymin, "From the Q&A of *Shaykh* Al-Uthaymin," Archive of the Ahl Hadith Forum, *Al-Maktabah Al-Shamilah Al-Hadithah*, 325, accessed June 1, 2024, https://al-maktaba.org/book/31621/34827 p50.

Our Shaykh Muqbil b. Hadi al-Wadi'

While studying in Dammaj, a student married and invited the *Shaykh* to his *walimah*. Initially, the *Shaykh* excused himself as he had visitors. After some insistence, we convinced him to attend and bring his guests. The next day, the *Shaykh* and his visitors attended the *walimah*. Everyone enjoyed the festivities, and before departing, the *Shaykh* made *dua'* for the newlywed.

During the *Sahih Al-Bukhari* class, the *Shaykh* regularly called upon students from various regions to stand and recite *hadiths* from memory. The day after the *walimah*, it was the Western students' turn. So, after several students recited, the *Shaykh* sought out the student whose *walimah* he had attended the previous day. The student was sitting behind a large pillar—out of the *Shaykh's* view—feverishly trying to memorize the narration. The *Shaykh* called on him again. He stood. He made a few attempts but could not get past the first two narrators in the chain of transmission. A wide smile came across the *Shaykh's* face, and he said, "It was said long ago, 'Knowledge has been lost between the thighs of women.'" The *Shaykh* laughed, and the students erupted.

Shaykh Hammad al-Ansari

Shaykh Hammad al-Ansari said, "I prayed in al-Quba Mosque, and upon leaving, I encountered a Ph.D. I knew well. When I greeted him as '*Shaykh*,' he grew upset, saying, 'Do not call me *Shaykh*, for the term has lost all meaning. While in Makkah, I witnessed an old woman shooing away a dog, calling it '*shaykh*.' This incident led me to avoid the title. I earn my living as a Ph.D., so I prefer to be addressed as such."[1]

Also, 'Abd al-Awwal b. Hammad al-Ansari said, "I heard my father repeatedly tell young married men when they were not eager to seek knowledge, 'The *Salaf* said, "Knowledge has been lost between the thighs of women.""[2]

---

[1] *Al-Majmu' fi Tarjamah Al-Allamah, Al-Muhaddith, Al-Shaykh Hammad b. Muhammad Al-Ansari* (2/700)
[2] Ibid., 2/583

Shaykh Rabi' b. Hadi Al-Madkhali

Shaykh Rabi' related a humorous incident during a *da'wah* trip:

We traveled to Kassala in Sudan to give *da'wah*. All praise is for Allah. We lectured, and Allah allowed the people there to benefit. It is a small town, so we visited all the local mosques.

Some brothers from *Ansar Al-Sunnah* said, "There is only one mosque we did not visit. They follow the *Tijani* methodology, and we've never been able to enter because of their fanaticism."

I said, "We will go there and ask permission. If they permit us to speak, we will speak. If not, we will leave. Whatever Allah wills. We will not force ourselves on anyone." So, we went there, and the mosque's *imam* led the prayer. After praying, I greeted him [and said], "Do you mind if I give a small talk to these brothers?"

"Go ahead," he said.

So, I spoke, may Allah bless you, and called to Allah. I called to *Tawhid* and the *Sunnah*. I also refuted the mistakes and the misguided beliefs [of the *Tijanis*].

I continued until I reached the *hadith* of 'Aishah, which is agreed upon: "There are three things, if anyone were to relate them to you, he has invented a great lie against Allah. Whoever tells you that Muhammad has seen his Lord has invented a great lie against Allah; whoever says that Muhammad knows the future has invented a great lie against Allah; and whoever claims that Muhammad did not relate the whole religion to the people has invented a great lie against Allah."[1]

So, [the *imam*] got up and said, "By Allah, Muhammad saw his Lord with his very eyes."

I said to him, "May Allah reward you with good. ʿAishah, who is the more knowledgeable of his affairs, said that he did not see his Lord. And By Allah, if he had seen his Lord, he would have told her." He kept talking, so I said, "Wait until I have finished what I have to say. Then you may ask whatever you like. Whatever I know, I will answer. Whatever I do not know, I will say Allah knows best." I left him and continued speaking. Afterward, I was uncertain if he stayed or left.

Then, I heard one man in the crowd say, "By Allah, what this *ʿzul* is saying is the truth." *Zul* means "man" in Sudan. He said, "By Allah, what this man is saying is the truth." I stated, "Allah said…" and "Allah's Messenger said…" May Allah bless you. Then the *adhan* of ʿIsha was called, and I finished my speech. The *iqamah* was announced, and the people began pushing me to lead the prayer.

"Never," I said, "the *imam* should lead the prayer."

"By Allah, you lead the prayer!" they said.

"Fine," I said and led the prayer.

After the prayer, the youth from *Ansar Al-Sunnah* and I left the mosque.

---

[1] Refer to *Sahih Muslim* (no. 177).

"Where is the *imam*?" I asked.

"They threw him out of the mosque!"

"Who threw him out?"

"His congregation."[1]

[1] Rabi' b. Hadi Al-Madkhali, "*Al-Hath ala Al-Muwaddah wa Al-I'tilaf Wa Al-Tahdhir min Al-Furqah wa Al-Ikhtilaf*," accessed June 1, 2024, https://rabee.net/‫الحث-على-المودة-والائتلاف-والتحذير-من‬/.

Shaykh 'Ubayd Al-Jabiri

Years ago, some students of knowledge in Riyadh debated the permissibility of drinking non-alcoholic beverages like Barbican and Moussy. During that time, we visited *Al-'Allamah* 'Ubayd Al-Jabiri at his home in Al-Madinah. I asked him, "O *Shaykh*, some of our *ikhwah* criticize their brothers for drinking non-alcoholic beverages. Is this correct?" The *Shaykh* fingered the crease of his *shimagh* and replied, "Malik, go to the store, bring back some beverages, and pour them for us."

The *Shaykh's* humorous response clarified that consuming such drinks is permissible. Nevertheless, as students of knowledge, he cautioned us to be wary of drinking such beverages in public to prevent any misconceptions.

Shaykh 'Abd Al-Muhsin Al-'Abbad

While teaching the chapter of supplication in *Jami' al-Tirmidhi*, *Shaykh* 'Abd Al-Muhsin reached the *hadith* of Abu Hurayrah, who reported that the Messenger of Allah said,

إِذَا سَمِعْتُمْ صِيَاحَ الدِّيكَةِ فَاسْأَلُوا اللَّهَ مِنْ فَضْلِهِ فَإِنَّهَا رَأَتْ مَلَكًا وَإِذَا سَمِعْتُمْ نَهِيقَ الْحِمَارِ فَتَعَوَّذُوا بِاللَّهِ مِنْ الشَّيْطَانِ فَإِنَّهُ رَأَى شَيْطَانًا

"When you hear the crowing of roosters, ask Allah for His favor, for they have seen an angel. And when you hear the braying of donkeys, seek refuge with Allah from *Shaytan*, for they have seen a devil."[1]

During the explanation, the *Shaykh s* reader, 'Abd Al-Rahman Al-Rushaydan, came across a benefit in *Fath al-Bari*. He said, "Al-Dawudi stated, 'One can learn five qualities from a rooster.'" Al-Rushaydan paused before continuing. "Number five is a problem: 'having a beautiful voice, rising early in the morning, being protective, showing generosity, and...*mating frequently.*'"

The *Shaykh* smiled, and the students erupted in laughter.[2]

---

[1] Collected by Al-Tirmidhi in his *Jami'* (no. 3459). Authenticated by Al-Albani in *Sahih Jami' Al-Tirmidhi* (no. 3459).
[2] Abd Al-Muhsin Al-Abbad, "Explanation of *Sunan Ibn Majah*," accessed June 13, 2024,
https://www.alathar.net/home/esound/index.php?op=tadevi&id=8692.